SEPTEMBER
Song

LESLIE E. MOSER, Ph. D.

Star Song
PUBLISHING GROUP
NASHVILLE, TENNESSEE

Star Song Publishing Group, a division of
  Jubilee Communications, Inc.
2325 Crestmoor
Nashville, Tennessee 37215

Printed in the United States of America
First Printing, October 1991

Library of Congress Cataloging-in-Publication Data

Moser, Leslie E.
    September song / by Leslie Moser.—1st ed.
        p.   cm.
    Includes bibliographical references.
    ISBN 1-56233-027-6
    1. Aged—Religious life.   2. Aging—Religious aspects—
Christianity.   3. Christian life—Baptist authors.   I. Title.
BV4580.M58   1991
248.8′5—dc20   91-38914
                                                                                    CIP

98 97 96 95 94 93 92 91 — 8 7 6 5 4 3 2 1

Table of Contents

Preface

You and I are members of a special group of people. We who are in our 50s, 60s, 70s, 80s, or 90s have been blessed with a long life, but, sadly, that blessing may sometimes feel more like a curse. Many forces are at work to deny us the joy and the fulfillment that can come in these later years. That's why I am writing this book. I write to older Christians so that your joy in the Lord may be full.

I trust that I am addressing brothers and sisters who, despite our many differences, are experiencing some similar joys and frustrations at this stage of our life. This book is for and about Christians who are 50-plus and who are feeling distressed about growing older. My hope is that, as we grow older, each of us will still be growing.

Who Are the Aging?

About fifteen percent of Americans today are 50-plus. But around the turn of the century, that percentage is going to rise to about twenty-five percent, one-quarter of the country's population.

The baby boomers (persons born shortly after World War II) have already turned 40, and this group is large. Most of them will be 50-plus in fewer than ten years. I can't help thinking that they are really the ones who should be reading this book, and I hope they will. They might then avoid some of the things today's 50-plus Christians are experiencing; they might then be able to enter the last half of their life with optimism rather than despair. But you and I know that it's hard to think about getting older when you're young. You people who do read this book—whatever your age—need to know that it's not too late to profit from the new information coming from the latest research into aging.

Many Have Already Given Up

I realize that many older Christians will resist some of what I have to say. The reason is that the insidious and satanic forces of ageism already have their hooks in some of us. We feel nothing but despair over failing health and various catastrophic events both global and personal. Some of these events could have been avoided; some could not. Whatever our current situation or mood, every one of us will benefit by having a better attitude about ourselves and learning better ways of dealing with the challenges we face.

It may be difficult for you to understand my optimism. Even if you agree that we should look at the positive aspects of growing older, you may find that you just can't do it. Some of you, without thinking much about it, have let your disappointments and disillusionments become sharp spears of despair. You heard how terrible old age is, you believed these prophets of doom, you labeled yourselves "old," and now you have become your own worst enemy.

I want to change that. I want to help you overcome the obstacles you face and lay uncompromising claim to the abundant life Christ has promised to all those who believe—not just to the young. Life should become richer as we move ever closer to the day when we shall see Jesus in all His beauty.

Go Along with God's Plan

The difficult circumstances we face can sometimes make it hard to keep our joy in the Lord, but I want to help you accept God's challenge and use your God-given courage and determination to live down the gloomy prediction of a misguided society that idolizes youth. Our culture expects our golden years to be gloomy years. But we can rise above society's predictions, claim the Lord's promises, and experience real joy in Him despite the forces pushing us to despair. We will not give up the holy ground of joy in the Lord which is ours as brothers and sisters with and in Christ. Our God does not wish us to despair, not even for a moment. "Let not your heart be troubled," Jesus says (John 14:1). This is His wish for us, and it must be our command.

Leslie Moser
Waco, Texas
July 1991

CHAPTER 1

God's Great Gift
Life Now and Forevermore

⤜⤙

"I have fought a good fight, I have finished my course, I have kept the faith."—2 Timothy 4:7

⤜⤙

A few weeks ago I joined a neighboring congregation for its morning worship service. A large part of the music was performed by the young people of the church. Accompanied by guitar and piano, these young folk sang a number of lively choruses. When the congregation was asked to sing along, the words were projected onto a screen so that everyone could join in.

Heaven: Hope and Reality

My heart was especially touched by a catchy little tune some of you may know. The name of the song is "Say I Do," and the words go something like this: "Anybody here want to live forever? Say I do!" This song was clearly a favorite. As the congregation sang enthusiastically, I couldn't help but notice the people. Their faces were radiant with joy. It was an uplifting time for all of us, a time of celebration, a time when hearts were turned to Jesus, a time of worship within the body of Christ.

As a psychologist—and that title means, among other things, that I'm a "people watcher"—I am enthralled by peo-

1

ple. I easily lose myself in their actions and in their emotions. I study people and make educated guesses about them. Besides having over thirty-five years of experience teaching and counseling people of all ages from many walks of life, I served ten years as Professor of the Psychology of Aging at Baylor University's Institute of Gerontology. In the contemporary world of specialists, I am a gerontological psychologist. This focus on the activities and problems of mature people has caused this "people watcher" to focus especially on mature folk (I'm deliberately not using *old, elderly,* and *aging,* words which often sound so negative), and there were some mature folk in the congregation that morning.

And I'm sure that the mature folk—as well as their companions of every age—had no doubt that the question being posed in that little chorus points to the hereafter, to life in heaven, to life with Jesus. The members of the congregation certainly had their eyes fixed on heaven and were thinking about the gates of eternity opening wide to receive them, that they might be forever at rest in the arms of the Lord. Their zeal and commitment were evident in their voices and their countenances. That is the beauty of a heartfelt worship experience, particularly the music and especially the singing.

And the promise of eternal life is certainly cause for singing and joy. Jesus said, "Let not your heart be troubled: ye believe in God, believe also in me. In my Father's house are many mansions: if it were not so, I would have told you. I go to prepare a place for you. And if I go and prepare a place for you, I will come again, and receive you unto myself; that where I am, there ye may be also" (John 14:1-3). We Christians shall reside in that place He has prepared.

Living forever in heaven is the eternal hope of all Christians. And it is not just a hope, but a reality that brings untold joy to all of us in the body of Christ. Heaven is a biblical reality to which we may hold dearly and firmly.

Fixing Our Eyes on Jesus . . .

Many things passed through my mind as I shared this up-lifting time of worship with the congregation. I was reminded why we are admonished to gather on the Lord's Day. God wants to remind us of His glory, His power, and His love for us, and He does all this and more in worship.

During this special time of worship, I also noticed an inter-esting difference between the older folk and the younger mem-bers of the congregation. The older folk seemed more fervent, more joyful, and more expectant as they sang the refrain, "I do." I suppose I shouldn't have been surprised about this. So many of the folk in the pews who were enjoying the last third of their stay on this earth had fixed their eyes upon heaven, upon Jesus. They were holding on to God's promise that, one day, they would walk the streets of gold and experience the joys of fellowship with the Lord. These are among the most up-lifting thoughts we Christians can have. But let me suggest that fixing our eyes on the hereafter may inhibit the life we are now living.

Missing Joys on Earth

As I heard the "I do" sung and watched the faces—par-ticularly the faces of the older Christians—I wondered whether too many of the people were so focused on the promise of heaven that they weren't as much in touch with the present as they might have been. In my years of psychotherapy with folk who have entered into their "golden years," I have seen some become introverted and isolated. They look to the hereafter as an escape from experiences not altogether pleasant, from pain and sickness, and from frustrations with health, family, and fi-nances. In short, many of my clients were focusing exclusively on the hereafter too early and leveling out their lives too soon.

Is it possible that, in concentrating on heaven, many of us fail to maximize the joys available right here in this earthly life? I believe so. I also feel that we allow our zeal for telling others about heaven to diminish our productivity as Christians. We may think so exclusively about heaven that we fail to think about either how hungry millions of people are, how lonely our next-door neighbor is, or how beautiful the sunrise is here on Planet Earth.

Everlasting Life—Beginning Now

Let me tell you something that may change the way you think about heaven. I believe that this eternal life of which we speak and toward which we yearn has already begun. Today is the day of salvation, and now is the time to serve the Lord. Now we see through the dark glass—we don't see the Lord as clearly as we will in heaven—but at least we do see.

Think about it. Isn't it true that today, this day, is the first remaining day of your eternity? Eternity for you will not begin at death; it began the moment Christ entered your life. Christ came that we might have life. He does not teach us how to live in heaven. He teaches us to live on earth. His constant message is *hope* for the kingdom to come, but *help* for the kingdom at hand. We certainly should be exuberant about the reality of our heavenly abode, joyful about our heavenly fellowship with Christ, and confident in the promise that all things will be new. In heaven, we will see through the glass clearly; we will know Christ face-to-face.

The wisdom of the world, however, says, "Take heaven now." The idea (an unreasonably romantic one) is that this life is so perfect that there is no reason to wait for heaven. We already have it! The popular song declares, "Heaven can wait, just being here with you, breathing the air you do, heaven can wait." That is utter nonsense even if it is an acceptable song lyric.

You and I must keep looking forward to heaven—that glorious place where we will be able to sit at the feet of Jesus, that place which is down the road just past the milestone of death. But as Christians, we look forward to the joys of heaven at the same time that we embrace the joys of this life. Although life is filled with frustrations, pain, and misery, it is also a time for joy—joy not just because we shall soon be home with Christ, but joy that comes with living daily with and for Him. Our Savior came that our joy might be full even before we get to heaven, and we are to appropriate that promise daily!

Perhaps we can claim that promise and live it more fully when we look at death differently. Death is a milestone not on the way *to* everlasting life—it is a milestone on the road *of* everlasting life. Each new day, it is our charge to glorify the God who gave us our eternal life, an eternal life which began when we were born again. Search the Scriptures, "For God so loved the world, that he gave his only begotten Son, that whosoever believeth in him should not perish, but have everlasting life" (John 3:16). Belief in Jesus Christ means new birth and eternal life.

Consider, too, that none of the Scriptures which promise eternal life indicate that we must wait until death to lay hold of eternity. Eternity is guaranteed with our acceptance of Jesus Christ as Lord and Savior. Granted, a few Scriptures refer to eternal houses and mansions in the heavens, and so shall it be when we have passed the milestone of death. But right now we need to remember that Jesus is the way and the life (John 14:6). At the moment we accept Him as Lord and Savior, we receive the gift of eternal life.

Growing in Joy

Growing older brings with it many problems. Some of us have failing health, some have broken families, and almost all experience body aches, heartaches, or both. Adversity should never be the glue that holds us in relationship with the Lord. On the other hand, adversity should never separate us from the love of God nor from our joy in the Lord.

Is your joy in the Lord waning? Are you allowing despair about your aging to get between you and the Lord? If your answer to either question is yes, then you would do well to say, "Get thee behind me, Satan." This command applies whether you feel that Satan is a personal demon intruding in your life or if you think of your own personal weaknesses as an evil force. As you move through life toward heavenly fellowship with the Lord, your joy should become more and more full, even if your joy must sometimes be clouded by a film of physical or mental pain. And be aware that Satan will do what he can to minimize the joy the Lord would have you experience.

Growing Closer to God

Gerontologists and psychologists interested in the behavior of aging persons have done many careful studies on the religious activities of older persons. Let's look at what they've found.

First, they have found that, as people pass their seventieth birthday, they begin to withdraw from human contact. Now this statistical average may not describe you at all, but it is interesting to find that at least in England, Canada, and the United States, folk begin to "disengage" from others beginning at about 70.

Researchers are finding that people maintain approximately the same social contacts (including worship and church-related activities) until about age 50. Then, between 50 and 70, there is a shift toward more formal church activities and reduced social contact of other types. Some people believe that these studies show that folk become stronger Christians as they grow older. Well, maybe—if you use religious activity as the only measuring stick.

On the other hand, some researchers say that this increase in religious activities comes because the children are gone and people have more time for activities of all sorts, including church and religious activities. I think it's only natural that people find more joy in the Lord when they are not as worried about children, finances, and so forth, don't you?

Research shows that the average Christian experiences fuller joy in the Lord roughly between the fiftieth and seventieth years. What happens then? Research focusing on persons 70 or older indicates a decline in formal religious activities, and this is generally understood to mean that these folk are infirm or unable to attend worship services for one reason or another.[1] However, after age 70, there is a large increase in "personal religious practices" such as prayer, Bible reading, and thinking about the everlasting kingdom.[2] Furthermore, there is an increased dedication to "clean living" and, most of all, to thinking about others and the meaning of life.

Certainly, the elderly have more time to think about and do for others, but that is not likely the full explanation. The evidence suggests that persons over 70 have less dedication to ritual and less concern for counting how often they themselves—or the people around them—perform the "required" religious practices. Their personal relationship with God becomes more important to them, and their joy in their Lord becomes more personal and meaningful as well as more private.

Also, as Christians become older, they seem to find the chasm between this life and the next life much more narrow. They become more ready to make the short step from physical life to a new and different life. They joyfully step across the narrow chasm to everlasting life.

Seeing through the Glass More Clearly

In a beautifully-expressed theory of religious faith, Dr. J. Fowler identifies six stages in the development of faith. He calls the sixth and last stage "universalizing faith," and this last stage is seldom achieved by Christians under 60 years of age.[3]

Fowler believes that only as we move into the 60-plus years do we begin to see through the glass somewhat more clearly; only after age 60 do we come to know Jesus as well as we can this side of heaven. After passing the milestone of physical death, we will of course be able to see Jesus with total clarity, but it is the joy of older Christians to be able to see Him more clearly than younger believers do.

This journey into a deeper faith is the ultimate journey. The young, no matter what their merits, cannot reach the intimacy with Christ that belongs only to those who live long, have obeyed God's commands, and now rest in God's plan for their remaining days.

It's refreshing to see this greater knowledge of God in action, and I often see it in nursing homes. Some people were bigoted during their church-going days, thinking that their particular church doctrine comprised ultimate truth. They did not open their arms or hearts to everyone; they were not blind to race, color, or creed. But when they come together in nursing homes, evangelicals who have deplored Catholics all their life reach across that ideological chasm. Even the Christian-Jewish dichotomy often vanishes, and older people declare, "We all worship the same God." Jewish residents are often anxious to attend evangelical Protestant services in nursing homes. My wife, a pianist at these gatherings, tells me about Jewish women who sing "The Old Rugged Cross" with zeal and Protestant evangelicals who ask Catholic roommates to share religious symbols.

Do actions like these indicate the softening of brain tissue or incipient illness? Perhaps sometimes, but for the most part, I think this kind of reaching out illustrates godly love and a faith so deep that foolish sectarian divisiveness disappears in favor of universalizing and bonding faith. These mature believers are able to see through the darkened glass, and they see that many of the differences which have blocked Christian fellowship make no difference when one moves closer and closer to death on the way of everlasting life.

The Ultimate Victory: Life over Death

Sadly, not all of us begin to see through the darkened glass. If we are victims of our own pessimism, consumed by our pain and feeling despair about growing old, we will miss the joy which can be ours only after we have moved into this last stage of faith. It makes no difference what we call it. "Universalizing faith" is Dr. Fowler's phrase, but this greater intimacy with God just may be what the Bible means by achieving sainthood.

And it is definitely your choice to grow into this closeness with God, and you can do it. First, you must live long enough to achieve that special closeness. Second, you must keep your eyes joyfully upon the Lord, never allowing the despairing events of life to deter you or your own personal zest for life to wane.

I want to experience this kind of faith before I step across into the next stage of my everlasting life. Don't you? That closeness with God at this stage of our everlasting life is one aspect of God's great gift of love.

End-of-Chapter Questions

What do you most look forward to about heaven?
How are you experiencing a bit of heaven in your life right now?

How might you be "leveling out your life" too soon? (Where have you given up?) Where could you use an infusion of hope or new ideas about how to approach that aspect of your life you have prematurely let go?

Is adversity separating you from God or increasing your love and joy in the Lord?

Confess to God how you have let yourself move away.

Pray, "Get thee behind me, Satan."

Thank God not for difficult circumstances but for being with you in the midst of the body aches and heartaches you are experiencing.

How has your relationship with God changed through the years? Are you more or less involved in formal church activities? In private times of fellowship with the Lord? In regular Bible reading? How have you come to "see through the glass more clearly" and so know the Lord more fully?

CHAPTER 2

Living Old or Dying Young

❧

"O death, where is thy sting? O grave, where is thy victory?"—
1 Corinthians 15:55

❧

IT happens to everyone who lives long enough. IT lurks on the horizon—even for persons quite young. For many, IT is a nightmare already come true. IT causes pain, demoralization, the inability to breathe, and eventually a straight line on the oscillograph in the Intensive Care Unit. IT begins in the 20s and 30s like a low, ominous rumble of thunder. At 40, the rumble becomes more disquieting, and at 50 the storm breaks over many. No, IT isn't death, but there is no way to escape IT except to die. IT is aging. The optimistic use the euphemism "the golden years" while the pessimistic say, with head down and despairing voices, "IT is old age." Whatever IT is called, IT is inevitable for those who live. The message of this book, however, is that IT can be very good, even great.

Old Age: Gloomy Specter or Untapped Opportunity?

This despairing description of old age is terrifyingly accurate for untold thousands of people around the globe. Old age is an unspeakably horrible scene for many, as most of us know. We have the frail elderly among our family members and

11

friends, and we've seen the ravages of old age, physically aging bodies, and seemingly unavoidable disease.

If this horrible specter were death itself, then we could either fight it or accept it. Eventually, we would accept it, hopefully in the spirit of a risen Christ who asked, "O death, where is thy sting? O grave, where is thy victory?" (1 Cor. 15:55) Death has been conquered, but old age has not.

Ironically, the advancement of medicine has brought to many people extra days and years of suffering and indignity, and this is likely a reason for the heightened awareness of the frightening specter of growing old. People know that they can be kept alive almost endlessly even when all tangible reasons for living are gone. The media finds mercy killing, euthanasia, and the agonies of Alzheimer's disease especially attractive subject matter. True, these topics are newsworthy, but the over-emphasis of the negative to the neglect of the satisfactions, health, and good fortunes of most aging persons is producing near hysteria among untold thousands—and unnecessarily so!

The Power of Our Beliefs

I am convinced that the terrors of growing old are more mental and spiritual than physical. Many devastating aspects of aging are avoidable, if not correctable. They can at least be dealt with in ways that preserve human dignity, a positive out-look, and healthy self-esteem.

If I thought for a moment that the degradations of growing old had to remain with us or that we must all surrender to both the real and imagined horrors as they are described and lived out before us, I would lay down my pen. But I feel called by God to lead you out of the slough of despair and the night of your discontent as you live this last one-third of your life.

Basically, I refuse to believe that these horror stories must represent the facts of life for all or even for most of us—and I invite you to refuse to believe them, too. In fact, I'm convinced that the indignities of advanced age are necessary only for a limited few of us. They do exist—these gruesome realities of pain and uselessness are all too real for many right now. Often, though, these awful things exist only in our minds, demoralizing us and leading us to uselessness. We have been brainwashed to believe the worst about growing older.

As a psychologist, however, I believe that what has been erroneously learned or imagined can be unlearned and replaced by truth which can help us live life to its fullest. A meaningful life and a ministry to others is an attainable goal for all except a few frail persons. Many of our peers who could find meaning in life don't simply because no one has shown them how to be useful. Perhaps no one has encouraged them even to hope that they can still do something worthwhile. May this book be some encouragement.

Growing Old or Dying Young

Either we grow old or we die young, and that may seem like a no-win situation. But I believe you and I can be winners.

Death is inevitable, but some of us are able to say that death gives meaning to life. Perhaps, for instance, death motivates us to live fully and sometimes joyfully. The Epicurean philosophers insisted, "Eat, drink, and be merry, for tomorrow you may die." That's not exactly how we Christians think about life and death, but we do trust that God's plan for life and death is the ultimate wise one. But growing old? That just shouldn't happen!

Someone has said, "Death is God's gift, but old age is man's invention." And I agree. Each one of us invents old age. After all, old age is a state of mind, an attitude. The phrase "old age" certainly doesn't communicate anything about chronological age; that phrase is a comment on one's state of mind. We all know people old at 40 and young at 90.

So if it's possible to be young at 90, why are people so appalled at the prospect of growing old? If death is a gift, why would one's later years be so bad? Part of the reason is that we are living at a time when, as never before, getting old has been given an ugly image. The sociologists call this attitude "ageism."

The Worship of Youth

You don't need me to tell you that ours is a youth-oriented society. Everything good is everything young. We worship lean and trim bodies, bright eyes, and unwrinkled skin. Advertisers select youthful models, and those over 40 try to imitate the lifestyle of people in their 20s. The media applauds youth and portrays older people as pitiable shells of nonpersons who have few, if any, redeeming features. With that image held out before us, why would anyone want to grow older?

Dispelling the Myths of Aging

Thanks to the media, people of all ages are being inundated by many false and misleading ideas about aging. As a result, perhaps for the first time in history, young people have heard a lot about their own aging process. Certainly, there are positive aspects of this. It is, for example, good that people think ahead about their lives and plan constructively. When many people look ahead, however, they are devastated by the great number of myths concerning old age. In this the youth-oriented culture, everyone thinks young is good and old is bad.

Consider the stereotype of people approaching their sixtieth birthdays (even their fiftieth, in the eyes of many). They're slow-minded, dim-witted, and forgetful people bent over with arthritis or osteoporosis. According to the mythical stereotype, the bodies of older people are wracked with pain and disease. (Indeed, old age itself is seen as a disease!) Other myths emphasize a disappearing sexuality, living the last years of life in a nursing home, and spending the final days in abject poverty. These people are expected to be cranky, burdensome, and often borderline vegetables. It's not hard to understand why, with this kind of publicity, many people are convinced that the last years of their life—perhaps as many as the last thirty—will be void of meaning and utterly hopeless.

Sadly, elderly people do find themselves in the kind of hateful circumstances I have described, but my description does not represent the situation of the great majority of us. To the contrary, only about five percent of people over 65 live in nursing homes. The level of poverty among people over 65 is no higher than that for the population as a whole. Both men and women can and often do maintain active sexual lives into their 90s. Reliable research suggests that most elderly people have a satisfying life.[1] Despite these facts, many people, young and old alike, still refuse to see the positive. Instead they focus on the worst possible scenario for their future. And these worst-case scenarios are reinforced at every turn. Healthy, well-adjusted, happy, old people are not newsworthy. The media go for the gruesome, the gory, and the heartbreaking stories of the little old bag ladies.

Statistics on Aging

Government documents from the National Center for Health Statistics and the U.S. Bureau of the Census show the following: It is not until age 75 that over fifty percent of the population are physically or mentally limited in any way. Of that fifty percent, only twenty-two percent are limited to the point they cannot carry on a major activity. Even at 85, no more than sixty percent need assistance in personal care or home management activities.

As I've mentioned, people are living to be much older than ever before. By the year 2000, twenty percent of the population will be 55 and older. By the year 2010, this will number jump to twenty-five percent, and those over 65 will represent about fifteen percent of the population. By the year 2050, one-third of the population will be over 55, and twenty-five percent will be over 65. The "graying of America" is an undisputed future reality. It remains to be seen whether or not the "despairing of America" will occur also. It need not.

Life Expectancy

In 1900, the life expectancy was 47 years. In the early 1990s, life expectancy for white females—that segment of our population which lives the longest—is 76 years. (There is a small variation in this life expectancy for males and for ethnics.) Most elderly people express a high degree of satisfaction with their life. And this important fact contradicts the myth of aging that says the elderly are miserable, sick, and depressed. Some certainly are, but that need not be the outcome of your life or mine.

Look again at the numbers. People 40 years of age may expect to live for another thirty-five to fifty years. Statistics compiled by the American Council of Life Insurance show that, on average, a Caucasian female who was 40 in 1990 can expect to live for forty-two more years. Many of us will live longer, and some much longer. A large portion of people in their 70s are still extremely active. In light of these statistics, it seems that 50 or 55 could be considered middle-aged.

Acting on these statistics, sociologists have redefined the aging population, breaking it into two groups. Those people aged 65 to 85 are the young-old; those 85 and older are the old-old. It is generally agreed that the young-old may continue in productivity and activity until their 85th year. People older than age 85 tend to experience fast decline and death.

Some authorities predict that, not many years hence, 85 will be the average life expectancy and almost everyone will live to that age. But with age, one must expect a rapid decline. Even now, though, some people live to be 100 or more, and a few even live to be 115. (Actually, 115 years is said to be the end of the human life span, but the idea that no human will ever live longer has been attacked. Researchers have suggested that breakthroughs involving the human immunological system may extend the 115-year life span.)

Right now, the fastest growing segment of our population is people over 85, and from this point on, the population will continue to grow older. Certainly, I am not suggesting that living longer is the ultimate goal. Living better longer may or may not be.

The Nation's Shifting Power Base

Living better is already an issue for those of us in the last one-third of our life, and it soon will be an issue for a large segment of our population. The baby boomers of the forties and fifties are now approaching and passing their fortieth birthdays. Soon they will be among the young-old. Hopefully, this aging of the American population will mean that the nation's power base—the command generation—will shift to the young-old group and that the young-old group will make an effort to protect themselves as well as the old-old group which many will eventually join.

Concerns about Growing Older

Understandably, people who are relatively young are becoming anxious about the years which lie ahead. Some are worrying about rampant crime, fearing that they'll never live to grow old. Others are worrying about whether they'll have any way of surviving if they do grow old. Will the Social Security check be there, or will the system be bankrupt? Can I save enough money to make it when prices are skyrocketing? Can I get my kids through college?

The main worries are probably more personal. What's going to happen to me? Will I be happy? Will I even have a reason to live? Some people would say that these people need to trust the Lord. After all, He gave them all these extra years, so He'll see them through. But some people—and I'm one of—them feel that trusting the Lord requires that we act as we trust and, in this context, prepare for our older years. Reading this book will give you some ideas.

Early Retirement

Despite the legitimate concerns people have about growing older, many people feel the unmistakable pressure to retire early, even as early as 50. Even though mandatory retirement has been raised to 70 and may soon be abolished altogether, records show that very few people are staying on the job until age 70. Early retirement seems to be the rule rather than the exception. (See Chapter fourteen for a more thorough discussion of retirement.)

In 1935, Social Security determined that 65 was "old" and the age to retire. Now, in the 1990s, people are retiring at 50 or 55. Remember, though, that between 1935 and 1990 our life expectancy has increased $11\frac{1}{2}$ years, so a person who is $76\frac{1}{2}$ in 1990 is at the same point in his life as the person who was 65 in 1935. Yet people today are not working until they're 76. Many are retiring at 55! We have many more years to live, but fewer of us are choosing to work during those years.

Living Abundantly

Today's life expectancy statistics suggest how unbelievable it is that people would retire at age 50 in 1990. Why would they want to disengage completely from work and life when they have so many years still ahead of them? By disengaging at 50, they may spend thirty-five to fifty years in limbo. And if this trend continues, there may come a time when people have as many years after their major career as they did before they started their vocational journey.

While those of us in our 70s know about these realities, it is not easy for those of you who are 50 to grasp the significance of these changes. You may have many years after retirement. Will you spend them in hopeless dismay or will you make those years truly golden?

It's a pity when people of any age are unable to maximize their life. It is a sad reality that people in their 50s—those who are beginning to experience "aging"—must change their attitude before they'll be able to enjoy life. The last one-third to one-half of our life can actually be fuller, richer, and more meaningful than ever before.

The Tragedy of an Unwanted Life

I remember Aunt Sue and Uncle Joe. They were my favorites when I was a teenager. I went fishing a lot with Uncle Joe, and Aunt Sue made the best blackberry pies in the world. She could be a little contrary at times, but those spells didn't last very long.

These two devoted Christians and beloved family members

were about 70 and I was about 50 when they celebrated their fiftieth wedding anniversary. On that day, Uncle Joe, hale and hearty, vowed he'd live to be 100. He even joked about what kind of woman he wanted as a second wife. Aunt Sue said that was all right with her because, with her arthritis, she wouldn't last much longer in this life. She said, "I hope the good Lord takes me home soon. I've had enough of this world." She really meant it, too.

What happened to these two good folk? We buried Aunt Sue a month ago. She was 92, and the last twenty-two years of her life were miserable for her—and for everyone who came in contact with her. She whined her way through twenty years, and never did a day pass that she didn't express the hope that the Lord would take her that very night. A virtual invalid for her last ten years, Aunt Sue seemed to cause everyone (and one of her daughters in particular) unreasonable and unnecessary misery.

And what about Uncle Joe? He died of a heart attack at age 72. Uncle Joe didn't live the robust life of a hundred years he so fondly dreamed of, but maybe that's not so terrible. The fact that he so fervently wanted to live helped him love life while he had it.

But Aunt Sue! Dear old soul, she hated every minute of her twenty years alone. She never wanted to live them in the first place. That has always seemed such a tragedy to me, but it was God's plan for her.

Now I'm 72. I hope I'm like Uncle Joe—enjoying life until the day the Lord takes me home—and I'm going for 100 if He'll let me!

Great Expectations

When he was 80 years of age, the poet Oliver Wendell Holmes made the following statement: "There are two kinds of people who live to be 70 years of age. The first kind expect to live until they're 90, and the second kind expect to die. For those who expect to live to be 90 and who die it makes no difference; for those who expect to die at 70 and live to be 90, it is hell."

Without apology for Mr. Holmes's language, let me say that he makes a very powerful point. To update his statement with 1990 data, we would have to begin with, "A person who gets to be 90 comes in two types . . . ." But the reality that Mr. Holmes expressed for people who were age 70 in his time applies to even younger groups of people today.

We might with total candor say, "Some people approach their fiftieth birthday expecting to become useless and miserable while some expect to live to be happy and useful until they are 100. For those who live to be 100 and who are miserable for 50 years, *that* is unthinkable."

Are you expecting to become useless and miserable as the years go by? Are you living out these expectations?

Or are you expecting to be happy and useful? What are you doing to live out these expectations?

End-of-Chapter Questions

Twenty years ago, what was your greatest concern about growing older? Is that fear now a reality? If not, what does this suggest about the publicity aging has received?

What positive examples of aging do you see in the media (advertising, television programming, newspapers, magazines, film, etc.)?

Review the section on myths and stereotypes. Think about people you know and write their names next to the myth which their life dispels.

How is your life more abundant and more meaningful today than it was ten, twenty, or thirty years ago?

Do you know an Uncle Joe or an Aunt Sue? Which one do you want to be like? Why? Which one are you most like right now? If you see you need to make a change, set yourself a goal to help you make that change for the better.

CHAPTER 3

Called to Contribute

⥈⥈

"Behold, what manner of love the Father hath bestowed upon us, that we should be called the sons of God."—1 John 3:1

⥈⥈

I define *spiritual* as "that which is of God," and I ask you to consider the implications of that definition . . . .

God created the world and everything in it, including human life, and He continues to be intimately involved with His creation. His glorification of human life extends from the days of creation (Gen. 1-2) to Elizabeth's joy over her friend Mary's pregnancy (Luke 1:42-45) to Christ welcoming the little children to Him (Mark 10:14) to His death on the cross by which He opened the door to eternal life. The honor God gives human life extends to the final years of our life.

Since life has been created and blessed by God (Gen. 1:31), I see our efforts to enhance life as a deeply spiritual matter. Aging challenges us to enhance the gift of life God has granted us. Aging, therefore, is clearly a spiritual matter.

Spiritual Realities

"Isn't it true," you ask, "that, while human life is a spiritual concern, the impairments of old age are simply physical realities with no spiritual significance? Besides, don't we have to suffer the torments of the damned in this life in order to inherit the kingdom of heaven? Aren't old age, senility, and pain biological and social realities designed by God to prepare us for the releasing power of death?" The answer to these questions is both yes and no.

First, emphatically yes! All of life is sacred. Consequently, any attempt to celebrate, prolong, or make meaningful life on this earth is a spiritual proposition. But emphatically no! Our place in heaven is not related to the amount or length of pain, isolation, abuse, or meaninglessness we may suffer before our death. Jesus suffered on the cross, and through His suffering, we all were redeemed; "with his stripes we are healed" (Isa. 53:5).

We are, however, called upon to take up the cross and follow Him (Matt. 16:24). The Christian who understands that much suffering has meaning does not always ask for the easy road. In fact, we Christians are often called upon to suffer for our Savior's sake. Tertullian said, "He who fears to suffer cannot be His who suffered," and Peter wrote, "For it is better, if the will of God be so, that ye suffer for well doing, than for evil doing" (1 Pet. 3:17).

Is Suffering for Its Own Sake Redemptive?

Suffering for suffering's sake has nothing to commend it, but suffering for the glory of God affirms the redemptive suffering of Jesus Christ. We who are believers are required to glorify and celebrate His life, whether or not we are suffering. Adversity, pain, and frustration, in and of themselves, assure nothing, least of all God's pleasure in us. Christ opposes senseless human suffering, alienation, and abuse.

Furthermore, God does not require pain, depression, or guilt as a condition for eternal life. Suffering and anguish in this life are the results of sin and not a means by which God

24

assures us of a heavenly abode. Faith in His Son is all that is required for everlasting life.

Don't Believe All You Hear

Our society values youth and devalues the elderly, but God is no respecter of persons or ages. In God's economy, chronological age has nothing to do with a person's worth, and that's in sharp contrast to the way the world evaluates individuals.

Sometimes, though, even in our youth-oriented culture, we hear in sermon, speech, or song that the elderly have earned the right to reverence. After all, the line goes, we've parented the young, contributed to the country's economic stability, fought the nation's wars—the list goes on and on. Without wishing to be irreverent toward the elderly (after all, I'm a member of that select group!), I must say that I don't think we—as a group or individually—deserve any such praise. We did what we did out of motives that were not always as pure as the driven snow. We were simply doing our jobs, rearing our children, and making a living. We deserve no special credit for what we have done or are doing, and we should desire no sympathy or respect based simply on the number of years we've been around.

At the risk of appearing a bit belligerent, I must tell you that this praise from our youth, our politicians, our ministers, and even our peers should not become a focal point of our lives. What we have done we have done. Besides, I am afraid all this gushing covers over some people's hidden agendas. Couldn't this be the message behind the apparent reverences? "You've done well, old man/woman. You'll never know how much we appreciate you. Thank you very much. Now go quietly into the dark night. Approach thy death as one who lies down to pleasant dreams."

Can you see these words as basically a con job pulled off by people who may not even know they're conning us? These well-meaning folk are citing the cliches of the past, not realizing that, with the increase in life expectancy and myriad other factors, we mature adults have much more to offer them than sedate advice. We are not dim-witted and decrepit. Our value to society and God's kingdom will be as great as we choose to make it! Not only has our value as persons not decreased with age, but our value to society and the Lord's kingdom may very well have increased.

Have I indeed been overly belligerent? If so, it's only because I want to rally you to contribute to the world around you and to the eternal kingdom of God.

The Generation Gap

We who are older know our worth as persons, but the younger generation doesn't always see it. The generation gap is very real. However, it behooves young and old alike to remember that we are all in the same family of God. There should be no animosity between generations, and we must do everything possible to minimize differences.

A recent Harris poll revealed the following:

1. More than four-fifths of family members aged 18 to 24 run errands for parents or grandparents and help them when someone is ill.
2. Even people aged 80 and over continue to provide support to younger generations in their families, with fifty-seven percent helping out when someone is sick and twenty-three percent running errands.[1]

The generation gap is real, but bridges over the gap are just as real. What are you and I doing to bridge that gap?

There Is a Reason

Hidden behind so much of the encouragement to revere the older generation is the attempt to remove the 50-plus person from the workplace and ease us into retirement. Do you know that fully functioning persons at 50 are being pressured out of their rightful roles as movers and shakers in business, service industries, manufacturing, and high technology?

Laws against mandatory retirement to the contrary, people are being shunted out of active lives earlier and earlier. Actually, it doesn't take much effort. We don't even put up much of a fight because we've already become our own worst enemy. Too often, we've believed the myths about aging and the hollow praise from younger folk, and we step aside at the slightest suggestion that we should. Again, let me say that we needn't do that. We can and should continue to be involved in life.

At this point, let me close this short chapter with a reaffirmation of human worth. Every person is worthy because the Lamb who died for each one of us is worthy. Jesus Christ "who, being in the form of God . . . was made in the likeness of men" granted special worth to our humanness (Phil. 2:6-7). And that worth does not diminish with age. In the spiritual realm, our worth never diminishes. In the marketplace, it need not diminish for a very long time unless we want it to. In terms of national survival, we dare not concede a diminishing value for the elderly. Our worth can continue, it must continue, and it will continue!

End-of-Chapter Questions

What does the fact that God took on the form of man in Jesus Christ suggest about the human body, even an aging one?

Much suffering has meaning. How has suffering had meaning in your life? What have you learned from your suffering about God, about people, about yourself, or about what's important in life?

Should people in the last third of their life be revered? Why or why not?

In your opinion, why does our youth-oriented society have a hidden agenda ("Go quietly into the dark night") behind its apparent respect for the older generation?

I maintain that the involvement of seniors is important for national survival. Do you agree with me? Why or why not?

CHAPTER 4

The Blessings of Old Age

"The hoary head is a crown of glory, if it be found in the way of righteousness."—Proverbs 16:31

Since the beginning, God has made old age a blessing. Consider the blessing one of the Ten Commandments: "Honour thy father and thy mother: that thy days may be long upon the land which the LORD thy God giveth thee" (Ex. 20:12). God applauds longevity as a virtue and a gift. Although He wrote in His master plan that every person will die, again and again He glorified long life as a blessing.

At age 99, God covenanted with Abraham that he should have a son by eighty-year-old Sarah and that Abraham would become the father of many nations (Gen. 17). Let me remind you that God is here for you and me right now—regardless of our ages—just as He was there for proud parents Abraham and Sarah.

Victorious Living until Death

Chronological age has nothing to do with victorious living. We can live in victory wherever we are along the path of life. A life that is not victorious, joyful, and meaningful is an affront to God and His plan for us. God granted us a long life so that

29

we might joyfully glorify Him. If you are bemoaning your adversities because you're growing old, let me tell you that God will not be any happier hearing about them than you are thinking about them!

Now I'm not trying to make you feel guilty if you're depressed about growing older. After all, you're entitled to decide whether or not you'll spend your life being depressed. Only you can decide how you're going to feel about your life. But I don't understand why you would insist on feeling sorry for yourself! Life can still be very good!

Yes, I know I shall die. Every person will. But this book is not about dying; that comes naturally. Rather, this book is about living, and living an abundant life requires some effort. Don't set your eyes on death; that is a mistake. Instead, own your mortality just as you own your immortality. Then, with me, turn your eyes to life. Turn your eyes upon Jesus who is life. He will help your life be very good.

God's Plan for Us

We are circumventing God's plans if we see death exclusively as the great enemy of life and if, as a result, we don't receive and experience fully His gift of abundant life. God's plan is not ours to question, but let me remind you that God's plans do sometimes change. He changed His mind about destroying Sodom upon Abraham's pleading (Gen. 18).

Has God changed His mind about human life expectancy? I believe that through His marvelous gift of science, He has extended our life expectancy beyond the three score and ten years which the psalmist writes about. Our life expectancy is increasing, and how can that be anything other than His plan? God's plan for life is unchangeable in some ways yet, in His wisdom, changeable in others.

Biblical Admonitions

It is clear from the Bible that we who are elderly are not elders in the sense of being singled out as religious leaders. The congregation of Israel had elders leading it, and this practice continued in the New Testament church. Men of good report were designated elders in the church, and in modern congregations, the term *elder* is used in several ways to designate authority, responsibility, and positions of influence and leadership.

Even though the elderly are not automatically elders in the sense of church government, it behooves us as older people to hear what God says about elders through Joshua, Peter, and the apostles. The most common opening phrase is "the elders which are among you I exhort" (1 Peter 5:1). Such references indicate that the elders were respected as people of wisdom, courage, and vision. Seldom are elders or the elderly told to "rest on thy laurels and take thine ease." For the most part, the instruction was "Teach the young, care for the widows and orphans, do this, and arrange that." True, the elders grew old and faint; even as Joshua "waxed old and stricken in age," so did they. But the record is clear, the elders were "doers" and not only "hearers" of the word (James 1:22). Disengagement from useful activity occurred only when they, like Joshua, were finally "stricken in age" (Josh. 23:1).

Old age can indeed be a time of blessedness. As we move closer to death, we needn't move away from our active involvement in life until we are stricken unto death. Old age is a time for being blessed and for blessing others. It is not a time for being only marginally involved in life.

A Great Time of Life

The phrase "golden years" need not be a euphemism. There is much to commend the last one-third of our life. Through our

31

varied experiences, we have learned a lot about how to live. At the same time, we face many difficult problems. We have aging parents to whom we have become as parents, and we are actual parents of our own struggling offspring. Our children and grandchildren may make unwise choices and behave in ways which do not make us proud. These are among the negatives we may be experiencing.

On the positive side, we have settled into some comfortable niches. For some of us, relative financial security has arrived. Also, most of us have learned to manage our worlds instead of being managed by the forces around us. And it is possible, even probable, that we have overcome some neuroses and developed a personal rhythm that fits with the flow of life around us. We have learned that getting upset over minor hassles doesn't solve anything, and so we enjoy a more relaxed attitude about life. We worry about those things we can do something about, and we do what needs to be done. So far as things outside our control are concerned, we are learning to let these just slip by.

Perhaps the above is an overly optimistic description. Most of us, however, probably find ourselves being calmer about the events in our world that we were in the past. And, at long last, many of us are really hearing God speak through His Word and trusting the promises which are there for us, promises like "My God shall supply all your need according to his riches in glory by Christ Jesus" (Phil. 4:19) and "God is our refuge and strength, a very present help in trouble" (Psalm 46:1).

A Poet's Perspective

Consider poet Robert Browning's perspective on old age from the poem "Rabbi Ben Ezra":

> Grow old along with me!
> The best is yet to be,

32

The last of life, for which the first was made:
Our times are in His hand
Who saith, "A whole I planned,
Youth shows but half; trust God: see all, nor be afraid!"

I hope that I, like the Rabbi, am living my life as the "whole He planned," not looking back, only forward. And may I like the psalmist hear God's blessing, "With long life will I satisfy him, and shew him my salvation" (Psalm 91:16).

End-of-Chapter Questions

As the lives of Abraham and Sarah reflect, God's blessings don't end once we're 60, 70, 80, or 90 years old. What new and special blessings are you experiencing right now?

Depression can happen to anyone of any age. Our attitude, however, can help determine whether we experience a temporary bout with depression or an ongoing depression. Are you choosing to look at the glass at your health, your financial situation, your friends, your family as if it's half-empty or half-full?

"Own your mortality just as you own your immortality." Explain what this statement means in your own words; write your explanation as a challenge to yourself.

"Old age is a time for being blessed and a time for blessing others." We looked at the first part of this quote in the first question. Now consider how you are being a blessing to others. Be specific as you make your list.

How are these years "golden" for you? See "A Great Time of Life" for ideas to help you start making your list.

CHAPTER 5

Adjusting Our Attitudes

‿◦‿

"For as he thinketh in his heart, so is he."—Proverbs 23:7

‿◦‿

Martha Greer was 78 years old last week. In their fifty-three years of marriage, she and her husband, Gary, built a good life together. Parents of five children, they enjoyed a heady state of affluence and a fine reputation in the Christian community.

Then something unbelievable happened to Gary. Some said it was sickness, but others thought Gary had become possessed by a demon when he fell in love with a much younger woman a gold digger, most of Martha's church friends called her. Several years before, Gary had started liquidating assets in ways most people would have thought legally impossible. Somehow, though, Gary managed jointly-held assets and community property (which Martha had half interest in) so that most of their money ended up in bank accounts in his name alone.

Then Gary filed for divorce. Under the no-fault divorce laws, Martha could do nothing. Gary got his divorce with no problem, and Martha was left with virtually nothing. Gary left her the family home, but as little money as his legal chicanery permitted. Then he married his child sweetheart, as the church ladies called her.

Needless to say, Martha Greer was crushed. She had no work skills, few assets, and a long, lonely life ahead. Absolutely no one would have predicted that all these indignities would befall this fine Christian woman.

Martha's story sadly illustrates that the only truly predictable thing about life is change. And certain changes profoundly affect everyone. Inflation, high interest rates, tightening job markets, and savings-and-loan scandals are wreaking economic havoc. Eroding morality, increasing crime, and the breakdown of families are other frightening changes affecting our society.

And no group is more threatened by change than we, the maturing and aging. We older Americans are becoming pawns in the economic and social games being played out in this ever-changing world. We find it quite challenging to maintain our sense of personhood and worth, to lead a meaningful life, and to contribute to our society. We must reorder our thinking, our attitudes, and our way of seeing and reacting to the world.

Sadly, however, many of us feel much apathy, malaise, and self-pity. Too many of us don't see how we can do anything to make a difference in our world, so we resign ourselves to a life of hopelessness and gloom. But I say we can make a difference, and I say we must try!

An End to Apathy and Idleness

Society cannot continue on its downward course, and we older citizens cannot continue in our apathy and idleness. In fact, the world needs to realize that older citizens—we who have raised children, worked hard to attain some financial security, and known this country in its days of strength and world prominence—will not sit idly by and allow the current state of affairs to continue.

Although we older Americans may see our advancing years and the state of the nation as stressful and frightening, we are beginning to marshal our forces. We must recognize that we have the power to make our own lives meaningful and rewarding and that we have much to contribute to this country and to the kingdom of God. We are watching the future of our country grow dim, and we are aware of how we haven't been treated as equal citizens. And we older Americans are not going to take it anymore.

If what you've just read seems overly assertive, it is. Unfortunately, such a coherent set of attitudes among us older Americans hasn't yet gelled. But that will only happen if we dramatize the realities and communicate the facts to one another. Only then can we solidify our forces. The disturbing evidence, however, is that a majority of us see our possibilities as limited, and our lives as static and uninteresting. We aren't yet doing very much to improve that situation, much less society at large.

"Old age is a bad scene. We'll wind up penniless and in a rest home," one despairing older person told me recently. To which I said, "That may be true, especially if you expect it to be—but it ain't necessarily so."

We become our chief enemy when we believe what we hear about old age, revel in the prediction of our own sorry state, and then live out that prediction. We have listened too often and too long to what the prophets of doom say about aging. The years of maturity, the so-called "senior years," old age— these have been seriously misrepresented as decadent, passive, and impotent. The picture that has been painted is false. Once again I challenge you to reassess the myths you've heard about aging. You may be surprised to see to what extent our attitudes constitute the real problem.

Age: Not Necessarily a Factor

During the last few years, aging has become a tremendously popular focus for researchers and writers. Much study has been done to determine whether or not older folk actually experience the conditions generally associated with aging. This study has revealed that many of the negative features ascribed to old age don't happen. We have been believing myths about old age!

Obviously, everyone grows older, and it would be ridiculous to hope that the advancing years would leave us completely untouched by the ravages of time. Indeed, we may be sure that old age will bring very hurtful changes. There will never be an argument about that. But many changes which have seemed unavoidable for aging people do not happen as predicted. Studies on the intelligence of aging persons have, for instance, shown that there has been much misinformation about the loss in intellectual and cognitive functioning that we will experience as we grow older (see Chapter eleven).

Researchers have developed an "average aging person," but you and I don't need to be like that average. Furthermore, we must take statistics about the capabilities of the average aging person with a grain of salt. We need, for example, to realize that aging persons change in intelligence person by person (my change will not be exactly like your change) and that, typically, those changes are not damaging until the onset of a terminating illness or other catastrophe.

Researchers have also looked at such areas as memory, physical decline, sexual capabilities, and the ability to perform physical and mental tasks quickly. New studies have exploded many myths and promised the aging person a rich and rewarding life. May this information encourage us to improve our attitudes about aging and about ourselves.

If we older persons allow the popular myths about aging to

go unchallenged and if we expect our later years to be what these myths forecast, then society in general and each of us in particular will live out a self-fulfilling prophecy. If society believes that we who are aging have nothing to offer, we won't contribute to a society which badly needs our wisdom and our knowledge. And if we ourselves believe that we are seriously declining with age, we will in fact decline.

Look again at those forces in our society which have cast a pall of depression upon many of us as we've passed our fiftieth, sixtieth, seventieth, or even eightieth birthdays. Recognize that many ideas about old age are erroneous, hurtful, and sometimes even vindictive. Assess the facts you've read about and the reality you know. Then decide that the years ahead of you will be the most productive of all.

Strength in Numbers

There is little doubt that society, often with our silent consent, has sold its older citizens out—has sold us out by labeling us "old." We have learned to respond with depression and sometimes horror to our very natural aging process. The largest incidence of suicides is among white males over 65 years of age, but many persons of advancing years find life extremely meaningful. They live out their years with a sense of purpose, genuine happiness, and real usefulness to society. In many ways, our mature years can be happier and more productive than many earlier spans of life. And those mature years will be our best years if we are determined to make them so!

Soon, in the United States, over twenty-five million citizens will be 65 years of age or older, and the nation can ill afford to lose the strength and ability of twenty-five million of its people. That's almost twelve percent of the population, a statistic which emphasizes our need to come together and act to improve our society as well as our own particular situation. With twelve percent of the population 65 or older, we older Americans will wield some very real political clout. Also, we can offer the kind of wisdom needed to move the nation forward, work out our economic problems, and insure a better life for generations to come. The senior voting bloc is destined to become a mover and shaker in the years ahead—but only if you and I organize and act.

The Methuselah Syndrome

Unless our attitudes and expectations about aging change drastically, we shall never be able either to utilize or maximize our collective power. We must shake the attitude which may well be called the "Methuselah syndrome," the tendency to act old because we have been labeled "old." Let me explain.

Various forces in society encourage us to feel old, act old, and stop living full, productive lives. In many instances, these forces which would convince us that we are useless people leading meaningless lives are doing so with a certain degree of maliciousness. In other cases, the intent, while not at all malicious, is hurtful nonetheless. The media exploits us with advertising schemes reminding us of the supposedly many pains of old age. We are coerced by the get-rich-quick schemes of entrepreneurs to buy various products they claim will correct the entirely natural decline that comes with age. One popular message, for instance, is that to be 60 is to be arthritic and therefore unable to do anything useful . . . .

Mr. Mason was 97 years old when he joined the talk group at the nursing home. He listened intently while my wife, Ruth, talked about how all of us can do something to help others. After the session he asked, "How can I help others, Ruth? I just don't know what I can do."

"You're a Christian, aren't you, Mr. Mason?" Ruth asked.

"I sure am!" Mr. Mason replied enthusiastically.

"Well, then, why don't you witness every day to someone in this home? I believe they'll listen to you. After all, you've been a salesman all your life!"

"I think I'll do it," he said—and he did. He didn't miss a day until he died a year later. He was happy, he was contributing, and, in my mind, he was a champion. What's more, he knew he was doing something important right up to the time when he went quietly to sleep and awoke when heaven's door swung quietly shut behind him.

The Political System Doesn't Always Help

Political forces have done a disservice to citizens with their demeaning programs which, while possibly well-intentioned, have produced a population of persons who feel older than they need to. The Social Security system, while exceedingly helpful, has also been guilty of forcing age upon people who otherwise would be productive in the workplace for many more years. Politicians made early retirement possible at age 62 and established unfair rules stipulating that we can earn only limited amounts without penalties against our Social Security checks. Mandatory retirement systems have been hurtful to some of us, and various aspects of the legal system are encouraging the able elderly to release their hold on meaningful work sooner than is necessary.

And organized religion, without really meaning to do so, has brought many of us to the point of fervently looking ahead for the releasing power of death even though we have thirty or forty more years ahead of us. We are being robbed of a meaningful present as we are urged to look intently to the eternal future. But we are living our eternal futures right now! We are living out our everlasting life in the present—and some of us are making a gloomy, empty mess of this stage.

Let's throw aside these depressing images! Let's break the

shackles of the Methuselah syndrome with which we have been bound! We must stand strong against those forces which—with their negative views of aging—are robbing many of us of our sense of meaning, our happiness, and our productivity.

The Spans of Life

During the 1950s, psychoanalyst Erik Erikson outlined eight stages of life, moving from infancy all the way to mature age and death. Erikson saw the eighth stage as a time of integrity vs. disgust and despair. In his view, at retirement age (55 in Erikson's framework), we experience either a sense of integrity or a sense of despair. If we choose integrity, we accept where we are in life and grow old gracefully. The stage of integrity Erikson described was the epitome of everything good for the older person, and it has many positive features which reflect the decade of the fifties when the theory was formulated.[1]

Certainly, even today, it is much better to choose integrity and see our life in a positive light than to sink into despair and despondency, making ourselves and those around us miserable. This concept of integrity is useful and affirming, but it is incomplete for those of us in the last decade of the twentieth century. Because we are living much longer now, we need new ways of looking at reality.

The New Eighth Span

I am proposing that we push Erikson's eighth stage to the ninth position and add something different as the eighth stage of life. I am calling you to reenergize the years of your maturity! I am calling you to a lifestyle that emphasizes continuing activity! The changing world, our increased life expectancy, and dozens of fresh new forces demand that the eighth stage of life be a time of forceful and meaningful participation in life. We need Erikson's concept of integrity, but integrity must be pushed ahead into a ninth stage. And this shift will demand from us a new level of involvement with life for our many remaining years.

Let's be honest. We know very well that a vast majority of post-retirement persons have not chosen ongoing and enthusiastic involvement in life. Instead, they have become victims of despair. And this pattern will continue unless we exercise the rights to involvement which are granted only to those who demand them.

Nursing homes are filled with persons who could be productive. How many persons are vegetating in nursing homes simply because they have nothing to do and no other place to go? We don't know exact numbers, but we can guess that there are many.

We also know that few persons choose depression and a loss of vitality because they really want their life to be that way. But our society of throw-away goods also has its throw-away people. Ageism is a problem that will be solved only if we who are being relegated to a meaningless existence will stop listening to false prophets, will unite, and will demand and obtain what is rightfully ours—the chance to be actively involved in a meaningful life.

Disengagement theory holds that older people fare better if they disengage from work and save their waning strength for the certain assaults of disease and death. This scenario may have seemed appropriate, satisfying, and the ultimate of everything good to the maturing person of thirty years ago. But not now! And I seriously question whether or not we can surrender our involvement in life when there is no one more able to contribute than we. I am convinced beyond a shadow of a doubt that disengagement from life serves no healthy purpose. Disengagement brings weakness, not strength; meaninglessness, not fulfillment.

The eight-stage span of life has long been a useful metaphor, but with newly-emerging realities, the metaphor needs to be re-shaped to take into account the many years that have been added to our life expectancy. True, life will end, but the beginning of that end should not be determined by some arbitrarily-selected event or randomly-chosen age. We must realize the truth—the best part of life on this planet lies ahead for many of us!

As you've undoubtedly noticed, I am convinced that old age is basically a state of mind and that our decline until we contract some terminating illness is more myth than fact. That's why I will continue to encourage you to find ways to maximize your life.

Solutions

How can we escape the Methuselah syndrome, that tendency to act old because society says we are old? How can we muster the courage to challenge the forces that are trying to make us feel old? We can do so by being smart.

Many of the factors which cause physical breakdown in the latter years are controllable. Nutrition, for example, is very effective in keeping older persons active and productive. Good health, a reasonable goal for any person at any time of life, is a must for the aging person. I cannot overemphasize how important our health is. We must invest energy and effort in our search for solid nutritional practices, good exercise programs, new surgical procedures, recent developments in medicine, and helpful self-management practices which can keep us alert and productive. Among the many guidelines for maintaining health and vitality which are easily available to us are diets, exercise programs, and self-care tips relating to our principal enemies—cancer, heart disease, diabetes, and arthritis. We need to take advantage of these resources so that we can be the resources to society that we are capable of being.

Time Wasted Is Time Lost

True, older persons have been sold short by the political and legal systems. But laws can be changed. Regulations can be put in place in some instances and abolished in others. The status of older persons can be made secure by appropriate political and legal action designed to protect and enhance the lives of persons entering this new eighth span of life, and the Older Americans Act has helped. In a sense, it is now up to us older Americans to act. If we don't make the effort, we will have no one to blame but ourselves.

All of us must, of course, grow older. Time is ultimately the great enemy of our earthly life, but many enemies can be defeated when we recognize and confront them. Although we shall never be able to defeat time, we are victorious over it when we live life to the fullest. We need not allow ourselves to feel or act as if we are half dead when we can be totally alive. Isn't it abysmally sad that people are giving up on life at age 50, 60, or 70? Yes! Especially when people are living well into their 80s and 90s! As I said, time wasted is time lost.

Pioneers and Messengers

Somehow we must let people in their 30s know that life doesn't grow sour simply because the body grows old—but we can't convince the young until we convince ourselves. Also, we must realize that what we do now to enhance our mature life will impact our children and grandchildren. We must be role models because, if we aren't, they won't know how to be productive during their golden years. We must be the pioneers in this new wilderness; we must wrest meaningfulness and productivity from this unexplored domain. We are entering an era where the average person will live 85 years as compared to 47 years in 1900 and 76 in 1990. We have never before been in this territory. Those of us now in our late maturity must clear the way for those who will follow.

And why must we? Simply because there is no one else who can accomplish for God and for our country what we can accomplish. We were the power base of the '60s and '70s, and we must continue to be. It is good for us to continue, and we can continue. We must make the world understand that active, meaningful, productive life does not necessarily end or even wane at age 50, 60, 70, or even 80. Most of all, we must be communicators of the good news that God has given us extra years on this planet. We are now spending a few more years of our everlasting life here on earth. Thanks be to God that our extra years on earth take nothing away from our time in heaven!

Champions

Who among us should be counted as champions of the mature years? Are champions found only among those continually healthy, virile, fully-functioning individuals who continue their outstanding successes into their 70s, 80s, and 90s? Is a president of the United States who functions exceptionally well in his 60s and 70s a champion? Is a 78-year-old heart surgeon working fourteen-hour days in life-threatening emergencies a champion? Is a 92-year-old minister, who is still active in campaigns of worldwide evangelism, a champion? Of course these people are! But so are wheelchair victims if they are expectant and enthusiastic about life.

45

Be a Champion

One group of researchers has described champions as the "armored personality."[2] Elderly persons with this personality are achievement-oriented in their attempt to stay young. The armored personality's neurotic striving is, however, a defense against their greatest fear the fear of growing old. This group of researchers sees the armored personality in a pitiable light, but I say better to be armored and neurotic than disintegrated and despairing! We must not believe that the man or woman who seems armored is necessarily neurotic. Work and involvement can be a defense against despair or an offensive thrust toward meaningfulness. Let me illustrate.

George was the youngest person in the nursing home. Perhaps he shouldn't even have been there. He was slightly brain damaged, and his mother had cared for him all his life. When his mother died, his relatives had a physician certify him for nursing home care even though he had almost no disabilities.

When Ruth met him in a talk group at the nursing home, George was bored and frustrated. He sat close to Ruth because she reminded him of his mother, whom he sorely missed. He talked to Ruth about his boredom and the hopelessness he felt being there "with all these old people." George desperately needed something to occupy his time.

Ruth had an idea. She asked the director of the home to let George sort and deliver mail. George was completely capable, and he became very proud of the job he did. Now, after four years, he is very possessive of his responsibilities. He wakes up thinking about his important position, and everyone hails him as the mailman. He conscientiously asks people if they're getting their mail. George will likely be a successful mailman for the rest of his life. He gets no pay, and the state inspectors actually frown on the possibility that management is manipulating a patient. But George is happy. He has a reason to live. He loves the old people now and serves them in a variety of ways. Yes, George is an "armored" compulsive and constant worker, but he isn't neurotic. George is immensely happy. He has found his niche. George is a champion.

In contrast to the "armored personality" is the "integrated personality," a self-assertive personality relatively free from aggressive or defensive feelings and actions. Whether or not that is a healthier personality, it is the personality of the majority of maturing champions. You are not a champion only if you are healthy, vigorous, and productive. Champions of the eighth span are known by their attitudes as well as their actions.

So, is the cancer-ridden person, who smiles her way through intractable pain while she faces each new day with much courage and some joy, a champion? Is the person, who has become more pleasure-loving simply because that's the way he wants to live, a champion? Of course they are!

To be fully alive to every opportunity and fully able to make a choice regarding those opportunities—*that* is a mark of the maturing champion. What one chooses to do with one's life does not determine a champion. The true marks of a maturing champion are his or her values and the attitudes that stem from those values. So long as our love of God and our commitment to Christian values are our first priorities, we can all be champions!

End-of-Chapter Questions

What changes in your life, in society, and in the world situation have made these years different from (and perhaps even better than) what you expected? Be specific about how your life is different from what you expected and note the tone of your words. What is your attitude toward these changes?

What might we older Americans gain if we work together to exercise our political clout?

Remember Mr. Mason, the salesman-turned-evangelist? What special ministry can or do you have now? God uses us for His kingdom, whatever our situation in life.

What are some of the serious consequences of the disengagement theory? (See "The New Eighth Span.")

Describe a maturing champion you know.

With what attitude does he or she approach life?

In what activities is he/she involved?

What ministry does he/she have?

How does his/her life reflect Christian values and a love of God?

Now reread these questions and ask them about yourself. What does this look in the mirror teach you about yourself?

CHAPTER 6

Living with Health and Vitality

⌒‿⌒

"What? know ye not that your body is the temple of the Holy Ghost which is in you, which ye have of God, and ye are not your own?"—1 Corinthians 6:19

⌒‿⌒

We are told on good authority that human life expectancy is steadily increasing. While the average life expectancy for Caucasians was 47 in 1900 and 65 in 1950, it zoomed upward to 76 in the early 1990s. Every indication is that it will move even higher.

While it is both interesting and important that we are living longer, of greater import is the quality of that living and how to sustain our vitality with age. Who wants to live a long life but spend many of the later years disabled and in pain? Happily, people are not only living longer, but many are also living with continued vitality. And it's possible for all of us to do so!

Long Life and Short Decline

The best case scenario for aging is to live a long and meaningful life and then decline rapidly and die soon thereafter. The ideal would be to have human life take on the qualities of Oliver Wendell Holmes's "one-hoss shay." According to this story, the deacon fashioned for his parson friend a shay that would last not forever but for a long, long time. Then instead of

49

breaking down, it would simply wear out; it would suddenly disintegrate at a moment in time.

> "Fur," said the Deacon, "t's mighty plain
> Thut the weakes' place mus' stan' the strain;
> 'n' the way t' fix it, uz I maintain,
> Is only jest
> T' make that place uz strong uz the rest."

The one-hoss shay lasted many years without repair or breakdown because every part was made of equal strength. But when the shay went, it went.

> What do you think the parson found,
> When he got up and stared around?
> The poor old chaise in a heap or mound,
> As if it had been to the mill and ground.
> You see, of course, if you're not a dunce.
> How it went to pieces all at once.
> All at once, and nothing first,
> Just as bubbles do when they burst.

It is commendable to hope that one day we may have human bodies like that—bodies that are fully functional until they go and then they go completely and all at once. In fact, it may surprise you to hear that this aim is at the heart of geriatric medicine. Ideally, everyone will have a long, useful, and healthy life that ends relatively suddenly.

Right now, though, a reasonable goal for us is life without a painful or debilitating disease. Indeed, most infectious diseases have already been conquered, and gerontologists are saying that a disease-free life should end at an average of 85 years. Of course, no one knows what the future will bring, but for researchers, 85 is the hoped-for life expectancy. The number of persons living well past 100 may increase slightly while the number dying before 85 would likely decrease.

The Human Life Span

The prediction of a maximum life expectancy of 85 years is contingent on the idea that the human life span is fixed by the genetic code. The term "life span" refers to the maximum possible length of life. Every living organism has a genetically-coded maximum life span. Redwood trees at 2000-plus years may represent the longest span, but most authorities agree that 120 years approximates the oldest age to which humans may ever aspire. As of 1990, 116 is the oldest documented age of any person. (Let me just mention that many quite elderly people have a tendency to overstate their ages, especially in certain cultures.)

Perhaps Moses should be the prototype for people of advanced years. The Bible says, "And Moses was an hundred and twenty years old when he died: his eye was not dim, nor his natural force abated"(Deut. 34:7). Moses died at 120 with "unabated force." This certainly is a worthwhile goal for us twentieth-century humans. But, clearly, longevity is much less important than vitality.

Ideal Life, Ideal Death

Today, assuring life without disease that ends quite suddenly at about age 85 would be a magnificent achievement, and it is imminently attainable. In 1981, researchers suggested that 85 years was the maximum average life expectancy. At the time, the average life expectancy was only 73.[1] By 1990, life expectancy had increased by approximately another three years, and likely will continue to increase. Researchers have been surprised by how quickly the human life expectancy is increasing. Who knows? An average age of 90 may turn out to be more realistic.

But how can we maintain our vitality up to age 90 or beyond? In search of some answers, let's look for a moment at the road we've traveled to get to the today's 76-year life expectancy for Caucasian females.

Historical Perspectives on Infectious Disease

In 1900, the infant mortality rate was extremely high. Except for the period of infancy, death occurred almost equally throughout the life cycle. That high rate of infant mortality, however, kept the average life expectancy quite low. After about 1940, as the infant mortality rate declined, infectious diseases kept death rates throughout the life span about the same as 1900.

Until 1950 or so, there was not a sharp increase in life expectancy. The life expectancy has since increased, however, because in the last forty years infectious diseases have caused significantly fewer deaths.

- In 1900, 914 persons in every 100,000 people died from tuberculosis. In 1920, the incidence was down to 154 in every 100,000 people; in 1940, down to 46 deaths in every 100,000 people; and in 1970, down to two deaths in every 100,000 people.
- Typhoid fever deaths have all but disappeared.
- Pneumonia and influenza have been the most persistent diseases with 202 people in every 100,000 dying in 1900 and 31 in every 100,000 in 1970.
- Although diphtheria, whooping cough, measles, smallpox, and other infectious diseases still exist, fewer than one person in every 100,000 dies from any of these diseases in any single year.

The virtual elimination of most infectious illnesses has increased life expectancy dramatically. Accidental deaths by motor vehicles—the largest single cause of death among people under 25 years of age—account for twenty-seven deaths per 100,000 people each year. Accidents of all kinds represent the largest single cause of death across the entire population.

Protection from Infectious Disease

Until 1950 or so, medicine focused on infectious diseases. The vaccine for smallpox came in the twenties. Immunizations for diphtheria came in the thirties and for whooping cough and measles in the forties. Polio was brought under almost total control in the fifties. New generations of drugs—the sulfa group was first, followed by antibiotics beginning with penicillin—put the killer pneumonia within easy control. No longer did influenza or various other epidemics run rampant through a population.

New forms of infectious disease, however, will undoubtedly spring forth. AIDS, for instance, has become a scourge in the 1990s, but we have assurance—hopefully justified—that infectious illnesses will kill only the very weak and frail. Actually, Alzheimer's disease represents a great unknown in this respect. No one has discovered what causes it. Some researchers suspect that a virus is involved, but even they agree that the condition is not contagious.

Chronic Disease

Death from old age alone (natural death) is perhaps quite rare. One reason is that the infectious microbes still around attack weak and defenseless bodies. But there is a much larger reason why natural death rarely occurs. That reason is chronic or universal illness.

Chronic illnesses have been with us all along, but with infectious diseases first identified as killers, chronic illnesses were not brought under attack as soon. Besides, chronic disease was

considered largely unavoidable, so medicine focused on offering relief. That focus changed once the infectious diseases
were, for the most part, conquered.

Chronic disease usually begins early in life, builds up slowly
through the years, and emerges in an identifiable form some-
where along the way. For example, atherosclerosis (clogged arteries) begins as early as the twenties. Layer by layer, plaques
start to build up in the arteries. They multiply and, as the years
go by, block the arteries more and more. Many of us simply
don't live to the point where blocked arteries seriously affect
our health. In some people, however, this impeded blood flow
causes heart attacks, strokes, and other catastrophes or
discomforts.

The pattern of atherosclerosis is the pattern of all chronic
diseases. Unless we control the disease or delay its impact on
our bodies, those diseases will either kill us or render our body
weak and vulnerable to remaining infectious microbes. But, to
a large degree, we can prevent chronic illnesses, and we can certainly control their progress. With careful body management,
we need not die prematurely at 75 or 85 from chronic disease.
Still, few of us will die from old age alone. That remains the
optimal goal—to impede chronic illness until a person can die
of old age alone.

As I've said, infectious disease is largely conquered, but
chronic disease is increasing. And we can expect evidence of
chronic disease to increase as people live longer. We will, for
instance, no longer die before the plaques clog our arteries to
the point that they cause us health problems.

I've mentioned atherosclerosis. Other chronic diseases are
arteriosclerosis, cancer, diabetes, emphysema, cirrhosis of the
liver, and arthritis. Key to defeating these causes of untimely
deaths are prevention, early detection of the disease, slowing
its progression, and treatment with medication and surgery.

Chronic Diseases and Lifestyle

The medical world hasn't determined the cause of every chronic disease. It is clear, though, that cirrhosis of the liver is caused by alcohol consumption and rarely by anything else. Lung cancer and heart disease are often caused by the nicotine in tobacco. Most chronic diseases have been studied sufficiently to indicate probable causes and risk factors. Some chronic diseases, however, are probably completely unavoidable, coming to us from our parents. But even these genetic diseases can often be detected early and their effects delayed.

Medical experts suspect that most of us develop cancerous cells which healthy bodies reject. If the base cause of developing these cancerous cells is genetic, keeping our bodies healthy, strong, and able to reject cancers will allow us full life and natural death. Thus, the theory goes, strong and virile bodies can prevent cancer.

Besides helping to prevent disease, good health practices also slow the progressions of certain chronic diseases. Rheumatoid arthritis, for instance, can be controlled or slowed with medication. People may have the disease at some level for decades without it contributing to their death. In a sense, then, arthritis is prevented; that is, it is prevented from becoming the killing agent.

These scenarios should not be seen as gloomy prognoses. We have to die, and our death may occur because of old age or disease. Either way, we will have had our joys, done our work, and gone home rejoicing to live with the Lord.

Be Kind to Your Body

Living life to its fullest has more to do with vitality than longevity, and there is a happy set of circumstances here. Most chronic illnesses are products of lifestyle. We are certain that cirrhosis and many cancers are caused from bad health practices. In fact, most of the chronic illnesses occur as the body fends off insults made to it. When we consistently insult our bodies by working too hard, living with too much stress, smoking, drinking alcohol, using drugs, or getting insufficient sleep, our body will retaliate by developing chronic disease.

Fortunately, most—if not all—of the body's hostile reactions which cause chronic illnesses are reactions to our mistreatment of our body, mistreatment which is not pleasant to begin with. The body does not require that we be joyless and bored in order to be healthy. Our body does, however, react negatively to insults which are hardly ever pleasant to the person delivering those insults. In the beginning, smoking is a nauseating experience. It is only when we ignore our body's pleas for kindly treatment that our body reacts with hostility and chronic illness. Our body is imminently reasonable.

Your body carries on a dialogue with you that goes something like this: "Be nice to me while you're enjoying yourself, and I'll be nice to you. Insult me and you'll suffer from nausea or drunkenness—and I'll get back at you."

The Temple of the Spirit

Most of us abuse our body in one way or another even though our body is the dwelling place of the Holy Spirit (1 Cor. 6:19). That fact makes our abuse of our body sinful. And consider the contrast. When a valued guest visits us, most of us put our houses in order. We vacuum the carpets, dust the furniture, and pick up any mess.

But we don't always do that for the Holy Spirit. The Spirit often dwells in bodies which are unkept, unhealthy, and unfit. Ideally, keeping our body healthy means making it the best temple possible—and we'll benefit from that. So what shall we present to the Holy Spirit as a dwelling place? Only the very best our body can be!

Keeping Fit Is Mandatory

We have no choice. Whatever our age, we must dedicate ourselves to preserving our health, stamina, and vitality. Less than total dedication to physical fitness is an affront to the God who created us. He will accept nothing less than our best effort to keep physically fit. We glorify God when we are conscientious stewards of our bodies, our minds, and our spirits.

End-of-Chapter Questions

What factors (nutritional, medical, social, scientific, etc.) have contributed to longer life expectancies?

What are you doing to protect yourself from infectious disease? From chronic disease?

What are you glad you did in your 20s, 30s, or 40s to protect and preserve your health?

Outline your current exercise program. If you don't have one, work with your physician to develop one. You also might look at your diet.

If you are currently dealing with a chronic illness, what do you do to maximize your vitality and improve your attitude? What could you be doing? Your physician or support group may have ideas.

Letting Go and Reaching Forward

"But this one thing I do, forgetting those things which are be-hind, and reaching forth unto those things which are before, I press toward the mark for the prize of the high calling of God in Christ Jesus."—Philippians 3:13-14

Have you ever attended a high-school or college reunion? You were really amazed by how old your classmates had become, right? Well, how do you suppose they felt about you?

Are You Growing Old, Too?

Most of us don't recognize the aging process in ourselves nearly as easily as we recognize it in our friends and loved ones. And most of us aren't really trying to avoid reality. We may be reacting to society's dictum that old is bad, but many of us are simply too busy to notice the changes in ourselves.

At age 70, Bernard Baruch said, "I have always defined old people as those fifteen years older than I am," and his definition is both good and bad. The good part is that, if we don't feel old, we have a tendency to act younger than we really are. We also tend to feel good about ourselves, and why shouldn't we? Not feeling old helps us plan for tomorrow and keeps us enjoying the way we are living in the present. All of us need to feel wonderfully alive, and feeling older helps no one. "You're as old as you feel" is a truism which isn't exactly true, but I do prefer seeing people feel younger rather than older than they really are!

So what's bad about not feeling your age? Well, not feeling or acting our age can cause other people some problems. When you act the way you feel, friction may arise when you don't act the way other people think you are supposed to. Surely, you know elderly folk who disregard some of the declining abilities of their bodies. They wind up doing foolish things, expecting their older bodies to deliver younger reactions. Some people believe this is why we mature folk are bad drivers, but statistics largely fail to support that claim. Still, we need to be cautious. You and I can hurt ourselves when we try to do something which our bones and muscles are unable to do.

Making Allowances

As each of us grows older, we must respect our body, its strengths and its weaknesses. But a more important point is that we have to release some of our activities to the realities of change. Let me explain.

Change is universal, but not all changes along the highway of life are changes for the worse. Not at all! Everyone speaks of "growing old," but too often we overlook the word "grow" in that phrase. Change is fundamental to growth. Said another way, without change there is no growth.

It is important to know that as our skill or ability in one area declines, we may get stronger in another. We need never stop growing even though our bodies are in constant decline beginning as early as the mid-20s. Does that sound like a paradox? Well, it isn't! There's much more to each of us than our body! Whatever the state of our body, we can still keep growing in a variety of ways.

59

Life Is Growth

Modern psychologists see life as a growth process that extends from cradle to grave. Certainly, they don't mean physical growth or increased stamina—even though, in the best of circumstances, our stamina can be maintained well into our 70s. These psychologists do mean that we continue to grow in our spirituality, in our understanding of the universe and our place within it, and in our relationship with God. True, even the full, good life brings us eventually to death, one of the milestones on the road of everlasting life, but, for the Christian, death is a new beginning.

It could be suggested that the path of our travel through life is a little like the trajectory of a bullet. A bullet travels until it reaches its destination. As it moves forward, it loses speed, and the trajectory is downward with the pull of gravity. We humans grow ever forward, but unlike the bullet with its steady but slowing speed, we move forward in spurts. While arguably the speed of our growth may drop off in some ways as we grow older, there are other ways in which our forward and upward motion can change suddenly and unpredictably. Unlike the bullet, our movement forward comes in spurts with new insights and renewed growth in our relationships with God and people.

Change and Age

Change is one of the few absolutes in this life, and all of us change as we grow older. Our body, spirit, relationships, and situations change. Time alters our body, our attitudes, our insights, and our goals. Every phase of life, with its inevitable element of change, requires from us some degree of growing up and letting go.

How can we grow and not change? How can we change

without turning loose parts of our lives? Can we stay like children forever? We can't. Like Paul, we must say, "When I was a child, I spake as a child, I understood as a child, I thought as a child: but when I became a man, I put away childish things" (1 Cor. 13:11). Who would want to stay a child forever either physically, emotionally, or spiritually? But to become an adult, we have to turn loose our childhood—although from time to time we may let the little child within us come out and play.

Consider, though, that we don't suffer much when we give up being a child. In fact, our culture applauds the youth we become when we move on from childhood. Most teenagers yearn to be grown-ups even though they are often quite unable to leave comfortable dependence behind. But as we move through life, giving up things becomes harder. For instance, it is difficult to say goodbye to alma mater and college friends upon graduation. It is difficult for parents—especially mothers to see their children grow up and move out. But growth demands giving up certain things. Growing and letting go—the pairing is inevitable. We can't stand still and grow forward!

Are You Fully Grown?

Some early psychologists and psychiatrists charted the life stages of children up to and including adolescence. Freud claimed four stages of life (oral, anal, phallic, and genital). Piaget charted the cognitive stages of childhood development from the psychomotor stage through the formal-operations stage. In the view of these psychologists, once a person was grown, he or she stayed that way forever. Modern psychologists such as Erikson, Maslow, and Rogers, however, recognize that being "grown" is the beginning of growth toward becoming all that one can become.

As we grow older, we can keep growing. We can grow in

spirit and grace, in generosity and caring at—least, that's the way it should be. But even this kind of growing is painful, for it means losing our grasp on the familiar, the comfortable, and the safe. But this letting go is necessary if we are to live life to the fullest!

The Pain of Growing

As I've said, change and growth usually become more painful as life unfolds. Parents, for instance, pay a high price when they give their the last child to the university, to a marriage, and to moving far away. Yes, growing forward exacts a price.

But how much greater a price is exacted in refusing to grow! When we fail to let go of the past, we can find no meaning in the present and the enriching experiences of each new day.

Some of life's changes don't fit neatly with the idea of growth. The death of a child, a parent, a spouse; the breakup of a marriage; retirement; moving to less expansive and less expensive living quarters—are these not times for tears? Of course they are, so let the tears flow. But ultimately each of us must ask ourselves the question, "Do I try too hard to hang on to that which was, or do I want to reach out to that which is and might be?"

Bending But Not Breaking

Our capacity to change and grow will depend on our roots. Are we firmly rooted in the promise of God that He will never leave us (Heb. 13:5)? Can we, like the psalmist, declare, "God is our refuge and strength, a very present strength in trouble" (Psalm 46:1)? As Christians, we should be firmly rooted in our faith, and the strength of our roots should contrast sharply with the flexibility of our confident stance in a life that is complex and demanding.

We Christians can stand tall and straight like a tree planted by the river of life, our roots sunk into the Rock of Ages. That root system will nurture us and enable us to withstand the storms of stress, frustration, and pain. Unlike rigid towers which, despite firm foundations, break and collapse, we will be able to sway with the winds of time and not break.

Consider, too, that strength comes with constant resistance to stress, and change can be a source of real and strengthening stress. The challenge of change, with its requirement to turn loose those things that are transient, frees us from the past—frees us to determine what we really want and what we really must do with the earthbound segment of our everlasting life.

We must make a friend of change and challenge. Then we will be able to let go of the familiar, the comfortable, and the safe. We must give our full attention to that which lies ahead. As we let go of the loved ones who pass, the relationships which did not endure, and our disappointments in people and events, we give up our cherished illusion of safety. In return, we gain a greater understanding of self, of God, and of eternity. We can be still and know that God is God (Psalm 46:10); we can know, too, that God "is a rewarder of them that diligently seek him" (Heb. 11:6).

Leaning Forward and Reaching Out

Letting go of things that are no more is not an all-or-nothing proposition, but in a very real way, we do have to let go of the past in order to reach forward to the future. We must lean forward, ready to move ahead even before we fully know what we are reaching out to embrace. For each of us, the future is mysterious, but it will be a puzzle never solved unless we join with Paul in an attitude of forward movement and forward intent: "This one thing I do, forgetting those things which are behind, and reaching forth unto those things which are before, I press toward the mark for the prize of the high calling of God in Christ Jesus" (Phil. 3:13-14). Thankfully, it is not necessary for us to clearly see the entire road ahead before we launch ourselves into the unseen and unknown. Our God goes before us and beside us.

With that assurance, each of us—regardless of our age—must reach out to our world and to the people around us. Our capacity for reaching out must be halted only temporarily by our painful losses and the winds of change in our lives. Then we once again must offer the touch of a caring hand which is always an expression of love. After all, love unexpressed is love lost. If ours was a serving profession, we must now reach out and serve in new and fresh ways. Never to look back is not a Christian virtue, and never to look forward is certain death for our Christian witness and to our wellness of mind and body. Looking forward and reaching out. That's what we're called to do.

Making It Happen

We can't wait for something good to happen to us. We must make it happen. Our zest for life must not be permanently diminished by change or tragedy. When we've let go of our pain, we will again find again that zest for living and renewed meaning in our life. It happens when we look to God and discover opportunities to reach out in service to Him and His people. Each minute of life can be an unrepeatable miracle that makes the present rich. Living fully in the present makes the past meaningful and the future possible.

Let go of the past. Reach forward to future. Never lose your appetite for what comes next. Look to God and let Him show you what special service and blessings He has for us, His mature and devoted servants.

End-of-Chapter Questions

How do you not act your age? How do you feel when you act younger than you are?

What have been the most difficult periods of transition in your life? How did God provide for you during those times? Be specific.

What has been the most difficult thing for you to let go of in the last ten years? What growth has resulted from that letting go? What did you learn about God during this time of change?

"We cannot wait for something good to happen. We must make it happen." This week, plan to make something good happen in your life. Then plan to make something good to happen in someone else's life and act on those plans!

What are you looking forward to right now? If there's nothing, ask a friend, pastor, doctor, or caregiver to help you discover an event (even one which is part of your daily routine) to look forward to.

CHAPTER 8

Self-Esteem
A Gift for God's Children

⤸⤹

"For ye are bought with a price: therefore glorify God in your body, and in your spirit, which are God's."—1 Corinthians 6:20

⤸⤹

In an article directed to new parents, noted Christian psychologist Dr. James Dobson writes that the greatest gift parents can give their children is high self-esteem. His reasons for saying this are obvious. If children don't think positively about themselves, they will be unmotivated and unable to be productive and they'll lack energy and enthusiasm for life. It is critical for children, with their emerging personality, to gain a strong sense of self-worth and self-confidence.

And isn't this sense of self-esteem critical for all of us at any time of life? It is indeed. We can hardly garner enough courage to do battle with the world in all its complexity if, deep inside, we feel that we are no good. It is out of the heart—out of our sense of worth as a child of God—that righteousness and good works come forth.

We All Need Confirmation

In order to maintain a sense of purpose in this universe, every one of us must possess a degree of self-esteem. As children, our sense of worth first comes from a mother and father who constantly affirm who we are and what we do. During every stage of life that follows, we require confirmation of our worth from others and approval from God. Very importantly, we also need to be able to affirm ourselves.

When we feel our worth as children of God and firmly believe in our ability to live productively, we acknowledge God. Through our life, we worship Him who created our bodies, minds, and talents for His service. Self-esteem means self-respect, and both are rooted in who we are as God's special and unique child. God condemns foolish pride, but self-affirmation derived from a sense of our value as a child of the all-loving God glorifies the God who gave us life.

The Loss of Self-Esteem

How fragile is self-esteem! How life-destroying an unkindness can be if it causes the offended ones to lose faith in themselves! Losing faith in oneself can shake one's faith in God. Self-esteem is the product of the God within us; losing it is like losing God. Finding it again is like finding God again, for self-esteem in a very real sense is the heartbeat of human dignity. Is not self-esteem the linchpin of our very being?

Children tend to have a fragile sense of self-esteem. They may lose self-esteem when, because of a single failure, they receive a harsh and foolish reprimand. We who are parents must realize how fragile our children's egos are. We can literally crush them with our thoughtless and unkind words. While their recovery from well-intended scoldings sometimes takes only a moment, at other times the effects last a lifetime. We undoubtedly learned long ago which of our children required gentle handling.

Self-esteem generally grows stronger with age because, as we grow up, we find meaning and a sense of self through our endeavors. True, a large source of meaning for our life is God

Himself, but important sources of meaning are the tasks to be done, the children to be reared, the vocations to be pursued, the people to love, and the people to love us back. The presence of God in our life is the ultimate source of meaning in these activities, responsibilities, and joys. But meaning also comes when we are able to reach out confidently and become involved in the world. With healthy self-esteem and the appropriate acknowledgment of the Source of all gifts, each one of us can make a difference in our world.

As we grow older, however, it is not as easy to make a difference. With age, for example, self-esteem will dwindle unless the aging person knows how the loss of self-esteem happens and how to prevent it. We must sustain a sense of purpose and significance as we grow older. We must not give up the struggle to make a difference in the name of and to the glory of God.

The World of Competition

It is harsh to suggest that someone is robbing an aging person of meaning and self-esteem, but ours is a world of competition and that kind of robbery happens. Not every person who pushes you aside from your meaningful endeavors so that he improve his own lot is vicious. In fact, few probably are. Most are simply working to reach their personal goals and standards of success, and they honestly feel that the older man or woman should move along to make room for them. Of course these aggressive people are dealing with their own issues of self-esteem, but I maintain that young people can protect their self-esteem without trampling on the self-esteem of the elderly. Likewise, we older folk can encourage the young, helping them experience and maintain feelings of worth.

Whatever our age, we should not seek self-esteem at the expense of another. It should never be the intention of the aging to deny self-esteem to highly motivated younger people. At the same time, we elderly people would be ever so foolish if we didn't guard the gates to our own self-esteem and refuse to allow our meaningful roles in life be stolen. We cannot be so generous—and of course it isn't generosity at all—to feel compelled to move over so that someone else can have a place in the sun. After all, everyone can find an opportunity for significance in the world and certainly in the kingdom of God.

In his old age, David asked God to hinder those who sought to hurt him: "Let them be ashamed and confounded that seek after my soul: let them be turned backward, and put to confusion, that desire my hurt . . . . Now also when I am old and grayheaded, O God, forsake me not; until I have shewed thy strength unto this generation, and thy power to every one that is to come." (Psalm 70:2; Psalm 71:18) David identified these enemies as people who "hate me without a cause" (Psalm 35:19). Today's unthinking young people who seem to despise older persons and those entrepreneurs who seek to take advantage of the elderly are twentieth-century enemies who "hate . . . without a cause." We, too, can call out to God for protection and guidance. At the same time, we need to be aware and alert.

Let's Not Be Naive

Research has shown that intellectual skills usually begin to diminish in the 30s. Other research shows little decline until the 60s. But don't be misled. Any possible decline is so tiny as to be insignificant until serious brain degeneration occurs. Such degeneration seldom occurs, although we are seeing an increase in organic brain syndromes like Alzheimer's disease. For the sake of argument, however, let's say that you and I aren't quite as bright at 60 as we were at 20, but neither are we as naive. As a matter of fact, with age and experience, we should be much less naive than we were at an earlier age.

"What are you trying to say?" you may ask. Just this: As we

grow older, we are going to be pushed aside if we are naive enough to permit it. We are acting naive, for instance, when we aren't alert enough to know when someone is putting us down and—it doesn't have to be someone younger. If we know it is happening and just go along with it, maybe we're not just being naive, but stupid as well.

Storms against Our Self-Esteem

We might hope that our sense of self-worth will weather every storm of life, but a lot of things can rob us of our self-esteem. People aren't always the villains. Ill health, for instance, is a vicious attacker of self-esteem. Who can feel worthwhile when they are ill and in pain, not knowing if they will live or die? Then there are the storms of financial loss; the loss of loved ones; lost jobs, friends, homes, and security. It is unlikely that any of us can sail through life without having our sense of worth undermined or, from time to time, even shattered. The real test is our ability to rebound from temporary defeat and again embrace a life of meaning and purpose. "They" may get us down, but "they" can't keep us down!

The Forces That Attack Self-Esteem

Vigilance is the price of liberty and the price of maintaining self-esteem. You need to identify the likely attackers of your self-esteem. Only by knowing who and what they are will you be ready to protect yourself from these attackers.

Let me offer you a word of caution, though. It is possible to become overly sensitive, distrustful, or even paranoid. I want to assure you that not every person or every force is out to steal your self-esteem. As you and I grow older, though, we become more vulnerable to the following:

1. Getting older means giving up roles which have given us a sense of purpose for thirty or forty years. When we are forced to give up these roles, we are bound to suffer at least a temporary loss of self-esteem. The three main roles which disappear during the sixth decade of life are work, child rearing, and meaningful relationships. Even meaningful marriage relationships can depreciate unless we are vigilant.

2. In order to promote themselves, some younger people will trample on us. Our fellow workers may want to make us feel old and force us out of their way. Our children may attempt to magnify their youth by imagining that we are old and helpless. (Let me mention that adult children often attack their parents' self-esteem out of motives not even they themselves understand.) If young people succeed in making you feel old, then you'll certainly act old.

3. Professional people such as physicians, psychiatrists, lawyers, and even ministers sometimes see involvement with us as a barrier to their effective functioning. We may not be attractive to them as patients or clients. These people often see us as not worth their time even if we do have more money than anyone else. Some people will take our money but despise us because we took up their time. If we seem like a soft touch, we may even be taken advantage of by people older than us.

4. There is a burgeoning market for thousands of items designed to tap the pocketbooks of aging persons. Many of these products—ranging from special types of toothpaste to special types of condominiums—have been conjured up by creative entrepreneurs. Unscrupulous home-repair con artists are among the worst of this lot. Never doubt that entrepreneurs are out to get your money. Even if you can afford to let them have your money, you can't afford

to give up your self-respect in the process. Use what they provide, and rejoice with them in your comfort and their profit, but don't be the proverbial sucker. Being a sucker—and knowing that you are—is hard on your self-esteem.

5. Many people of good intentions enjoy helping you. So many times these do-gooders think of themselves as martyrs. They may be our children or close friends. Whoever they are, the name of this game is patronization. You and I must learn the difference between patronization and kindness. If what these people do for you makes you dependent or makes you feel old, then your self-esteem is in jeopardy. As the song says, "People who need people are the luckiest people in the world," but this is true only if we can do something for them in return. True, one day you will be dependent on others, possibly entirely so. But even at that point, your self-esteem will remain intact if you know you are not being made weaker so that someone else can seem stronger. You can become your own worst enemy if you foolishly decide to sit down in your rocking chair while you are still perfectly capable of taking care of yourself.

You are entitled to a good life, so enjoy it! But don't give up your capacity for self-management when you decide to take it easy. That isn't necessary. Stay on top of the decisions that affect your life. Such involvement will add to, not take away from, your enjoyment of life. Don't believe that taking it easy means you must surrender your own decision-making rights. If you decide you no longer want to be self-managing—and that is your choice—you are sure to lose some self-esteem.

Self-esteem. As a child of God, you can know of His love for you and your worth to Him. As an older and wiser person, you can know what to do to protect that sense of self-worth. And it's that healthy sense of self-esteem that will keep you living a meaningful life.

End-of-Chapter Questions

Through the years, what activities, relationships, or accomplishments contributed to your self-esteem? What are the primary sources of your self-esteem now?

What role in years past was most meaningful to you? Why? Spend some time now thanking God for the blessings of that role.

How are your adult children affecting your self-esteem? How are you building up theirs?

Practice some assertive statement that you can use to protect yourself from professional people, entrepreneurs, and do-gooders who might however unintentionally rob you of your self-esteem:

"I understand that you're busy, but I ask that you be more patient / thorough / generous with the time I'm paying you for."

"Your product / service sounds interesting, but I'm not in the market right now."

"Thank you for offering, but I prefer to do it myself."

What are some of your favorite Bible verses which remind you of God's love for you? Let these reinforce your sense of self-worth. Committing one or more to memory can help!

CHAPTER 9

Your Sexuality
To Have and to Keep

~~~

"Marriage is honourable in all, and the bed undefiled."—Hebrews 13:4

~~~

Human beings are sexual creatures, made male and female by God. And when God gave the command to Adam and Eve to be fruitful and multiply, God not only approved sexuality but sanctioned sexual behavior (Gen. 1:28). Sexuality is a part of who we are; sexual behavior is ours to enjoy as a gift.

Special from the Beginning

God decreed that fish, animals, and birds as well as human beings should multiply and replenish the earth, yet man and woman are unique (Gen. 1). We can indulge in sexual behavior for reasons other than procreation. Our sexuality was given to us so that we might have pleasure in the body of our beloved. Consequently, sexual desire is a relatively constant in both the human male and the human female. This is in stark contrast to females of the other species. Female sexual drive is for reproduction only in other mammals.

But God gave Eve to Adam as a "help meet" (Gen. 2:18), a companion to help meet his needs, and those needs include his sexual needs. God created in Eve a corresponding sexual drive

74

that she might not only meet her husband's needs but meet her own needs and experience her own pleasures as well.

That Man and Woman Might Know Each Other

Sexuality and sexual behavior were given to human beings for procreation, pleasure, the avoidance of loneliness, fellowship, and spiritual communion between husband and wife. Consider the biblical description of sexual intercourse: "And Adam knew Eve his wife; and she conceived" (Gen. 4:1). The expression "knew" implies a rich intimacy, close familiarity, and pleasure in the body of the other.

The current generation (especially the younger segment) is often credited with having fostered a sexual revolution. At long last, it is thought, human beings have freed themselves from the repressive shackles built up over the centuries which kept us from knowing the full joys of sex. This notion of how sex has been experienced in the past may or may not be true. It is quite possible that, in the beginning, husbands and wives had no inhibition about sex and freely experienced the joys of sex even more than today's liberated generation. We can't know about the distant past, but we do know that, for many generations, societal and moralizing forces did repress people's sexual freedoms. To a degree, we are escaping from those repressive forces, but it is not yet clear whether our escape is a blessing or a curse—or both.

Repression of the Older Person

Sexual repression, for good or for bad, was forced upon the general population in times past and continues to be forced on many of us today. Specifically, people of advancing age are still victims of sexual repression even though it's the end of the twentieth century. In fact, people over 50 are quite possibly suffering from a double stigma. First, younger people don't seem to understand that we have the capacity and desire to be sexually active. Second, some of us are still affected by those repressive ethics under which we were raised.

Males and females alike who were born fifty or more years ago probably internalized much of the repressive elements of the era of their childhoods. They grew up at a time when sexual behavior was closeted not in bedrooms, but in cloistered minds. The era was characterized by confusion about sex, prudishness, and a denial of the legitimacy of sex as an integral part of the marriage bond. The scriptural mandate that two become one certainly has many interpretations. Can we emphasize the spiritual and deny the physical?

Sexual Behavior through the Years

Statistics are readily available to show that there is generally a decrease in sexual behavior with age. Statistics do not reveal whether this slackening is due to physical causes, lack of interest, or society's codes of appropriateness. Changes in sexual drive and/or performance undoubtedly have many causes.

The decrease in sexual behavior should probably be viewed as many-faceted and perhaps even as inevitable and desirable. But the decrease of intimacy with one's beloved spouse is a different issue. Ideally, couples should grow closer as the years go by. "Sweeter as the years go by" is a musical refrain intended to describe the relationship between God and human beings, but it is certainly not inappropriate to apply the sentiment to husband-and-wife relationships.

The media does not suggest that, with advancing age, there is less sexual activity, especially on the part of males. Instead, books, television, and the movies would have us believe that there is just less sex within marriage and more outside it. Nothing should be farther from the truth!

So what is the truth? Sexual behavior is much more frequent among married men and women of any age than among spinsters, bachelors, widows, and widowers of the same age. And this statement, easily supported by research, is an important reality for married persons young and old.

Let us not be misled by the soap-opera scenario. Too often the media makes sexual behavior outside marriage seem quite attractive, but it certainly should not be that way. Promiscuous sex is both sinful and destructive. It blocks our relationship with God and it weakens the marriage bond. Still, the media continues to offer Christians and non-Christians alike the lure of promiscuous sex. But Christian principles based on Scripture strictly forbid such extramarital sex. The Bible clearly teaches that there should be no sexual behavior outside the marriage bed. No relationship can escape disagreements which sometimes cause anger and disillusionment, but these disagreements must be resolved under divine guidance and not used as excuses for moving outside the marriage for intimacy.

Sex in Later Years

The best prediction for what will be is what has been. Uninterrupted continuance of sexual intimacy with one's beloved is found most often among those who have looked upon their sexuality as a valuable part of their relationship.

Loss of sexual desire with aging is one of the cruelest myths about growing old, and if either partner has embraced this myth, then the sex life of both will be affected. As a result, one of the spouses may seek sexual fulfillment outside the marriage, and this is true even of Christians.

Some couples enter into their 50s or 60s with a sexual handicap rooted in their distant past. Too often, one of the spouses has various scars from childhood which have affected him or her throughout the years. These issues may cause spouses to approach sexual intimacy with aversion, and that aversion doesn't always fade as they grow older. In fact, the male or female spouse who has struggled with sexual intimacy through the years may eagerly seize upon age as an excuse to withdraw.

The Most Intimate Years

Young spouses just beginning their sexual relationship are often frantically driven to emotional excess. In part, this arises because of God's mandate, "Be fruitful and multiply." A degree of urgency is written into God's plan so that the world will continue to be populated. More than that—or perhaps as an offshoot of that—the powerful hormones in their bodies often drive young couples toward joyful lovemaking. Early on, the quantity of expression may sometimes seem more important than the quality of expression. Later, quality becomes more important, and that is only one reason why the golden years are ultimately the best for intimacy.

Marriage in the Later Years

Relationships are difficult to build and to maintain, and this is becoming increasingly true as the world becomes more complex. Today, spouses seem driven to enhance themselves, to have successful careers, and to create individual identities. As a result, relationships are often neglected. Male and female personality differences and the modern emphasis on the equality of husband and wife are further causes of stress marks and serious cracks in many marriage relationships. Today's horrendous divorce rate results, and recent research reveals that spouses at age 60 are divorcing at about the same rate as the general population.

Ken Dychtwald and Joe Flower, authors of *Age Wave*, tell of a seventy-eight-year-old woman who divorced her eighty-one-year-old husband when she learned about her increased life expectancy. She said she didn't want to be married to "that jerk" any longer.

Dychtwald and Flower speculate that women are more likely than men to find reasons to end a bad marriage after fifty years or so because the woman has a much longer remaining life expectancy. But upon realizing that they may live as much as twenty more years, men and women alike may decide not to remain in unhappy relationships.[1]

Sadly, when marriages do survive into the 60s and 70s, often the partners' lukewarm commitment seems to be based on their decision to "stick it out." The two stay in the marriage because they don't feel they have any other choice. It's a tragic reality that spouses in their later years sometimes seem more enemies than friends. Few marriages can expect to be so smooth that no hurtful conflicts will arise, but what a shame that spouses can't always forgive and forget.

A Case in Point

Jim and Susan Black lived quite happily together through the first five years of their marriage and the birth and growth of two beautiful children. Then Harry was born. Harry was an awkward, troubled child from the beginning. Although not mentally retarded, neither was he as bright as his siblings. Jim struggled to accept Harry; he had a hard time facing the reality that he had fathered a child who fell so far short of his hopes.

The details are unimportant; the results are tragic. Jim and Susan—who were bound together by a shared hardship instead of by mutual love, respect, and admiration—drifted apart. They became spiteful toward each other, and both had affairs during the most tumultuous times of Harry's growing up.

But now Harry has found his personal peace. Despite heavy odds against him, he has completed high school, found a good job, and married a lovely girl. Jim and Susan are proud grand-parents to Harry's little boy, and Harry offers more love and de-votion to his parents than do his affluent siblings. These two prideful siblings are not very supportive of their aging parents, a sharp contrast to Harry and his wife, both of whom adore Jim and Susan.

Jim and Susan, however, live in turmoil because of the hurts they inflicted upon one another during the years when Harry was growing up. They cannot forgive each other, although deep in their hearts they are lonely for each other and desper-ately need one another.

Variations of this theme are played out endlessly among older couples. Of course, it is utterly foolish. Will the casket of your spouse be the only thing to help you see the pointless-ness and hurtfulness of your lack of forgiveness? Sadly, not even a casket frees every spouse from the rancor he or she has long nursed. And what does that person gain? Nothing.

Games That Spouses Play

Adult children, who are alert enough to notice, often marvel at the way elderly fathers and mothers rip each other apart with malicious and usually unconscious games. In his book, *Games That People Play,* Eric Berne defines games as transac-tions between two people in which one or both have hidden agendas which severely frustrate and damage the person who is the "goat" of the game.[2] A wife may scold her husband for being late for dinner, knowing that he can't help being late. The husband, goaded by her tongue-lashings, may start being later than necessary. This causes still more severe railing which causes still more tardiness. This kind of double gamesmanship and the vicious cycle it establishes is played out with hundreds of different variations. Spouses may keep it up for years, not fully realizing what they are doing to one another.

If a marriage counselor had the opportunity to work with the couple described above, the two might be persuaded to talk to one another in the presence of the counselor and under the umbrella of God's love. The counselor's presence might help keep tempers under control and enable each spouse to understand the foolish games he/she is playing. With proper counsel, earnest prayer, and a committed love, the two might become much happier in their relationship.

Supporting Each Other

It would seem only natural for husbands and wives to support one another when life gets difficult, but such is often not the case. Husbands, for instance, don't always—perhaps not even usually—understand how menopause affects their wives. Neither are husbands always routinely or appropriately concerned about the empty nest syndrome since they don't experience it as severely as their wives do. At the point when children leave home, most men are still very involved in work.

Unfortunately, marital infidelities during the later years—while not the rule—are not at all that rare, and this is true for both husbands and wives. Indeed, marriage counselors are needed in the later years far more often than they are called upon. Many elderly couples are not motivated to correct problems this late in life. Besides, problems which have often been left to fester may have resulted in alienation, withdrawal, and apathy.

Sadly, this estrangement seems sharpest when elderly spouses are especially in need of each other's support. Communication suffers, and insensitivity thrives just when husbands could be most helpful to their wives and wives most supportive of their husbands. It is also true that many spouses do help, but not to the extent they could or should. I see this marital stress as an opportunity for the church to minister to its older members. The power of God ministered through the body of Christ offers the best available hope for strengthening marriages, whatever age the spouses. Christ and His love are sufficient for all needs, but His will and His love often depend upon human vessels.

Leave the Past Behind

As a rule, youngsters grow up, lead their own lives, and have increasingly less time for aging parents. This is as it must be and should be. When children move on into their own futures, their parents need each other as never before.

Please allow this writing to encourage you to see once again the beauty and dearness of your mate. You can do this with the help of God's spirit of love. Give up blaming, carping, demeaning, humiliating, and belittling your spouse. Rekindle the spirit of love and allow God to heal the wounds.

Return to Intimacy

In our younger days, most of us confused intimacy with sexual need. Indeed, sex was created that the two might become one in body in a spirit of communion. Sex should never have been merely a physical act, although we may forgive ourselves if it once was that. We can't, however, allow this misguided notion to continue into our golden years.

Sexual intercourse is more than physical closeness. In fact, sex should be the ultimate in intimacy, but it is certainly not intimacy itself! While saying that sex is not an absolutely necessary aspect of intimacy, we must not fail to recognize the importance of sex as an asset to intimacy as we pass the milestones of our fiftieth, sixtieth, seventieth, eightieth, or ninetieth birthdays. What a beautiful thing it is—older love (including sexual love) between spouses who have forgiven themselves and each other for transgressions through the years.

Sweeter as the Years Go By

Jesus' love grows sweeter as the years go by, and so should marital love! And it's happening every day—but it doesn't happen by chance. A sweeter love between spouses happens only when we work to make it happen.

And the love which results is worth the effort, the commitment, the forgiveness, and the compromising and adapting. It is worth the dedication, hard work, and sleepless nights. It is worth maintaining even in the face of harsh words, impatient demands, and abusive behavior which are sometimes inevitable as the health of one or both spouses crumbles in the late, late years.

Make the Most of the Best

Knowing that our days of strength and good health are limited, we must make the absolute best of the good years together. With the help of God, our new longevity—which is given by God and assisted by our own informed efforts—will mean that intimacy may last thirty or forty years beyond the time many couples call it quits. With our children out of the nest, we can channel our energies and focus our thoughts on loving each other. Most of us can expect to thirty to forty years of happy living and loving.

We cannot blame anyone but ourselves if we fail to enjoy the best—and sexual intimacy in the golden years can be the best! Again, let me say that sexual intercourse is not the goal, but it does serve as a the means for attaining a blissful oneness with one's spouse.

Just as God decreed that the human species should freely enjoy sex, He has decreed that this glorifying act of oneness and communion can be enjoyed into very advanced years. The brain is the most important sex organ, and the brain, to a large extent, can control human genitalia. The critical elements are our attitude and expectations.

It's the Closeness That Counts

Before we were 50, most of us were very frustrated if, on initiating a sexual encounter, we were unable to reach orgasm. The good news is that orgasm may continue to be possible for both male and female even into our 90s. But in the golden years, orgasm should not be the goal which spells "virility" for either the husband or wife.

During the advancing years, sexual closeness changes. Sexual intercourse as we knew it when we were 30 becomes less frequent, but that is no catastrophe. The orgiastic nature of sexual release (if any) will also change with the years, and that is no catastrophe either. Male erection and ejaculation will be different. Again, no catastrophe. Female orgasm will be different if indeed it occurs at all. Still, no catastrophe.

The catastrophe happens when many elderly couples choose to no longer press their bodies together in loving embraces. The tragedy is that elderly spouses stop embracing, lying together, caressing, and offering pleasant tactile stimulation to one another. In fact, many spouses have denied their need for physical closeness for so long that they may no longer even feel the need. What a pity!

The Gift of Touch

Society foolishly preaches that sex is inappropriate for the aging. Nothing could be more untrue. Older bodies and spirits have an even greater need for closeness as the years unfold. And with society's denial that older persons need sex comes the denial that we need any intimacy at all.

It's tragic that some people do not know that touching is for everyone. Nothing can take the place of the human touch. Older bodies yearn for human touch. Many people have denied this need for so many years that they shrink from the touch of hands, but that unnatural reaction can be unlearned. The very special touching which causes sexual stirrings is properly reserved for marriage—for all the years of marriage!

Human bodies never become so wrinkled, so shrunken, or so physically debilitated that they do not deserve to be touched. And we most often desire the touch and caress of someone in our own age group. Our society denies this principle. Today, older women desire much younger men and older men desire much younger women. But these phenomena must be seen for what they are: evidence of minds and spirits sickened by faulty teachings, unstable childhoods, unhealthy environments, and, ironically, a society which discourages continued intimacy between spouses in their later years.

The Act of Love

When Ann Landers asked her readers about how uninvolved in sex they were, some 35,000 people responded. According to their responses, sixty-five percent of the couples over 65 years of age reported that they no longer engage in sex or do so only infrequently. Seventy-five percent of those over 70 responded the same way. This poll is hardly scientific research. People who are negative toward sex are more likely to respond to a negatively-slanted question. It is, however, interesting to note that the printed letters indicated little sex, but a lot of cuddling. And that is important. Sex can be defined in many ways, and cuddling is one such way.

Sexual climax becomes less important to elderly people than

other forms of intimate playfulness. Still, it is likely that many couples cease full sexual involvement before they need to. Elderly couples who engage in touching, caressing, and cuddling should not hesitate to continue to orgasm. However, special knowledge should accompany sexual intercourse in the later years. The following points are important:

1. As women age, vaginal membranes become thinner and lubrication less adequate. Too much friction can be uncomfortable and sometimes damaging.
2. Males cannot sustain erections for prolonged periods when they are older. More stimulation is necessary for completion of the sex act.
3. There may be vast differences in the sexual appetites of husband and wife. Neither should impose his or her desires to the discomfort of the other. Each should, however, make special efforts to accommodate the needs of the other. Honest and earnest sharing of feelings is a must.
4. Many efforts at coital sex for older people will result in failure for both spouses if orgasm is the only measure of success. There is, however, absolutely no reason why orgasm should be the only standard. Pleasure without either person's discomfort should be the real measure.

Each spouse needs the other's affirmation as they give pleasure to one another. As long as mutual caring and affirmation are present, any intimate contact may be referred to as sex and, most importantly, as successful sexual performance. The loving caress is sexual if it causes sexual response. If it doesn't, it is still an important act of love. And those kinds of acts can be enjoyed, no matter what our age.

End-of-Chapter Questions

In your opinion, how has the sexual revolution been positive and negative?

How has sex been a gift for you through the years? Thank God for that gift.

Lack of forgiveness can hinder every aspect of a marriage relationship, including sexual intimacy. What long-held grudges or hurts are you nursing? Let God and/or a pastor help you release your spouse from the past. You'll be surprised by how that gift of forgiveness is a gift to yourself.

How do you define success when it comes to your sexual and physical relationship with your spouse? Are you being realistic? Are you being loving? Are you being overly cautious? Have your spouse answer these same questions and then talk together about your answers.

What aspect of physical and sexual closeness with your spouse do you most enjoy now? How has your mate become more attractive to you through the years? Write a short love note and share these thoughts with your mate.

CHAPTER 10

Fellowship
The Family and the Church

❧

"This is my commandment, That ye love one another, as I have loved you."—John 15:12

❧

What happens to people's social lives as they grow older? Many persons begin a gradual retreat from social contact. For most people, that social withdrawal begins when their children leave home. The tendency to withdraw gets more pronounced when the spouses leave their jobs.

Is it a good idea for aging persons to withdraw from the stresses of work and busy social lives? Will the energy saved help their tired bodies remain healthy and strong? My answer to both questions is an immediate and resounding no! But earlier in the century, the thinking was different.

Disengagement theory, regarded at first as a boon to the aging, began to surface in about 1935. Social Security legislation, which identified 65 as the point of having gained the privilege of not working anymore, grew out of disengagement theory. For good or bad, Social Security legislation has made it possible for aging persons to withdraw from work and, essentially, retreat from life. Unexpectedly, at the same time that older folk leave their job, they also often withdraw from responsibility and from active life. This pattern became so clear that, in 1961, it was claimed that "disengagement is normal during the aging process."[1] All this was a result of legislators ostensibly permitting aging persons to preserve their waning strength. After all, the theory stated, disengagement would make it possible for older people to look forward to longer and healthier lives.

Since 1935, sociology, psychology, and gerontology have largely debunked the theory that disengagement is beneficial. Countless studies have shown than disengaging from work, social roles, and physical activity brings decline, disease, and untimely death. The activity theory has replaced the disengagement theory, and now countless studies are showing that people live longer, happier, and healthier lives when, within limits, they continue to be active.

Social Disengagement

Disengagement theory turned out to be a ridiculous proposition, but disengagement from life continues to be a reality. It is difficult, though, to say which form of withdrawal comes first as a person ages. Some say disengagement begins when the breadwinner (usually the husband) leaves the work force. But usually, prior to this event, the parenting role has already been left behind. Inevitably, some social activity is lost when the children depart.

But even with an empty nest, socialization continues in families who are in the work force. Employment tends to engage couples and families with other couples and families. As a rule, bonds of friendship are better maintained between people who view each other as equals and who have common interests and experiences to share. When people give up their work and their parenting roles, opportunities for socializing decline. Aging couples find themselves staying home more and more.

Socializing with Family

Many aging persons derive tremendous benefits from social-izing with their children and their children's families, and spending time with one's family can be wonderful. Families, however, can't completely fill the void that comes from with-drawing from people one's own age. The children (now grown and with families of their own) typically have social networks based on their work and their parenting roles. Socializing with their elders is often done with some degree of disdain and dis-comfort. Keeping in touch with parents is often more a duty than a joy. (Actually, the grandchildren often enjoy the time with Grandpa and Grandma much more than the generation in the middle does!)

So it is an open question whether or not having children nearby is a social advantage. Certainly there are pluses and mi-nuses. But even if children are nearby, aging persons need op-portunities to be with members of their own generation. Family relationships will not completely meet the social needs of elderly people.

It's interesting to note the several studies which show that the morale of older persons who see their children often is not as high as those who see their children less. One reason is that children bring their problems when they visit, and older per-sons tend to worry and feel frustrated when these family trou-bles are shared.

No solid conclusions can be drawn about the value of social-izing with family, but is seems safe to say that satisfying family relationships are more likely to exist when the older persons have their own independent social resources and are not com-pelled to depend solely on family for social outlets. Further-more, people whose only social contacts are family members build unhealthy dependency relationships in both directions. Parents depend on children for social contact and their children depend on them for financial assistance and help with child care, two areas which can become quite burdensome to many aging persons. Clearly, parents can often pay a high price for their family social relationships.

Enter Christianity

Christian fellowship is becoming more important as the complexities of the social, economic, and occupational worlds increase. Obviously, there was never a time when such fellowship was not important, even crucial. Early Christians could never have survived had they not joined together in the bond of fellowship. The early Christians were persecuted for their belief in God and Jesus Christ, but with the bond of His love, they found love and fellowship in each other. In the local churches, early Christians found joy, fellowship, and support, all based on their common love for Christ (1 John 1:3).

Is It Better Today or Worse?

The fellowship of Christians continues to be a thing of beauty as well as a necessity. Even critics of the organized church and of Christianity in general profess amazement at Christian fellowship. These critics don't understand how Christianity is not merely surviving, and they marvel over the way the church grows and thrives. They shake their heads in disbelief: "How can this be? Why doesn't Christianity crumble?" Indeed, today's enemies of faith though different from those of the early church are more tenacious. The tools Satan uses to try to destroy the church of Christ are sharp and subtle, but still Christianity and its followers survive.

In fact, the church has become a haven for young and old, for people of every walk of life. People are flocking with great zeal to their churches, seeking a fellowship that cannot be found in country clubs, discos, gambling casinos, or social ventures developed by modern entrepreneurs. There is no other fellowship like that which grows out of love for Christ and one another! In part, the renewal of churches everywhere can be credited to godly folk who seek companionship, fellowship, and social contact that don't conform to the world's patterns of sex, violence, drugs, and a general flaunting of the laws of God. Society does not provide wholesome social outlets.

Aging in the Religious Community

The church offers wonderful social opportunities for young and old alike, but young people in high school and college have many other outlets for social energies. Young married people and parents also have social contacts through their jobs and parenting responsibilities. There is nothing wrong with social life outside the church even though these social contacts don't usually involve fellowship in and through the Lord. While Christian fellowship is irreplaceable, it is not the only wholesome and worthwhile social involvement.

But, as I've said, most of these social opportunities disappear with aging. Couples may maintain good social contacts through a variety of secular activities and clubs. Across the country, communities of older people are springing up, and these deserve praise for the social opportunities they provides. The American Association of Retired Persons is doing much in conjunction with government-funded programs to provide social contacts and outlets. And then there's the church.

Endless Opportunities

Many aging persons have no history of church involvement. Indeed, many older people get involved in a church for the first time when the church reaches out to them. In fact, the social needs of older folk present a fine opportunity for churches to minister to members of the community and to share with those people the good news and hope of Jesus Christ.

The lack of social contact and the consequent loneliness of later years are more traumatic for those who have lost spouses and find themselves virtually alone. The Bible clearly instructs the disciples of the Lord to care for the widows and orphans (1 Tim. 5:4). Again, the church can play a vital role in reaching out and welcoming into fellowship those who find themselves out of the mainstream of life.

The church, however, needn't become the last resort for aging folk seeking fellowship, companionship, and social outlets. Instead, if it is functioning according to New Testament commandments and imperatives, the church will be the first resort for believers and nonbelievers alike. It is a mistake to think of the family of God as excluding anyone. We can not exclude anyone from the family of God.

Congregations of baptized believers do have the right to feel a special fellowship in Christ toward one another. Sadly, some churches have tended to become exclusive, in subtle ways issuing invitations only to those who fit prescribed criteria such as race, social class, level of income, etc. Christ has said that anyone can come and drink freely of the waters of life (John 7:37). Surely, this invitation includes an invitation to fellowship on a social level.

The church is the body of Christ and there is only one body of Christ. However, the majority of New Testament references to "the church" refer to a group of baptized believers who teach, preach, and promote the kingdom from within a local body of believers. We are one body made up of many bodies, and we are to always welcome more people into our fellowship.

Reaching Out and Moving In

Churches can reach out with a social ministry to persons at every stage of life. Vacation Bible schools, sports centers on church property, fellowship halls where meals are served, and celebrations of life and the Lord are only a few of the possibilities.

And it is certainly appropriate that the church should provide facilities, leadership, and a clear invitation to involvement to those who are growing older. Church leaders must also be aware that many people will not be able to participate in programs scheduled on church premises. Outreach must also touch the lives of housebound, nursing home-bound, and hospitalized persons, to mention only a few.

The church hears in Scripture these callings to serve, and these callings are to be tailored to modern situations. But those of you elderly who feel abandoned, insecure, and alienated within the social realm should not wait for invitations, coercions, or pleadings.

In every sense of the word, each of us is a person of choice. If you are feeling alone and out of touch with people, don't wait for someone to reach out to you. Your calling is to move into a fellowship which is waiting for you.

Many of you know very well that the church fellowship is there waiting for you just as the Savior waited for you to open the door to Him and to salvation and eternal life. You must find the courage within yourself to act—and then act! Return to your church if you've left it; become once again a part of the body of Christ.

Make the First Move

Don't grudgingly await the pleas and pressures of active church members. We can all sit at home feeling rejected, smug in the thought that it is the church's duty to coerce us back into the fellowship. We humans are amazing creatures. We often wait for others to do what only we ourselves can do—and the days and years slip by. By doing nothing except wait, we hurt only ourselves.

Yes, it takes courage to move toward church involvement on your own, especially if you are basically a shy person. Since life treats some of us rather harshly, it is only natural that we develop some self-pity and, with it, a reluctance to do for ourselves what we know would be very rewarding. We wallow in the morass of our long-term hurts, our egos often bruised from a single incident when we were sinned against. If you were sinned against at one time, that sinner must deal with his or her actions, and you must ask yourself, "Am I hurting myself with my unforgiving attitudes? Am I holding onto old grievances for all the wrong reasons?"

If you are living a joyless life, it can be joyous again. You can return to fellowship—fellowship with the perfect Christ and with His imperfect followers.

End-of-Chapter Questions

Looking back over the years, do you see a pattern of disengagement in your life? Why or why not?

Evaluate the socializing you do with your children. Consider the frequency, their attitude, your expectations, your stress level after they leave, and any dependencies which are developing. Is it time for a change?

Who are the primary people in your social network? Where did you meet them? Are those spots still a place for you to meet new friends?

How involved in a local church are you? What joys does this involvement bring? What opportunities for ministry? Thank God for the blessing of your church family. By the way, do you know someone you'd like to share that blessing with? Why not invite that person to go to church with you!

If you're not involved in a church, what is standing in your way? Are those obstacles insurmountable? What would you have to do to overcome those obstacles? Do it!

CHAPTER 11

Keeping Your Mind Sharp

⌒⌒⌒

"And Moses was an hundred and twenty years old when he died: his eye was not dim, nor his natural force abated."— Deuteronomy 34:7

⌒⌒⌒

Do you think as quickly and as sharply as you did when you were 20? Most folk over 50 would say, "Of course not!" And that is really sad because most of these folk are probably thinking just about as well as they ever did. It's a myth that getting older automatically makes you slow down intellectually—and, sadly, that myth is widespread.

I must absolutely insist that, as the song says, "It ain't necessarily so." Getting older doesn't always mean slowing down intellectually. But if you think you are losing your brain power, then you will lose it to a frightening extent! As the Bible says, "For as he thinketh in his heart, so is he" (Prov. 23:7). You simply can't maintain your sharpness when you yourself are convinced that you're losing your brain power.

None of us should expect to be like Moses whom God allowed to live 120 years without any decline in any part of his body. Growing old is bound to change our bodies, and we must expect that. When we expect changes, however, we learn how to live with those changes. Actually, we've been doing that ever since we were born, haven't we? We weren't the same at 28 as we were at 18 or 8 years of age. Furthermore, change is not necessarily bad, and there is no reason for us to think that the changes in our bodies later in life will all be bad. Some changes may be bad, but some may be good. And whether they're good or bad depends a lot on our attitude.

Intellectual Decline with Age: Myth and Reality

There is a great deal of debate about how aging affects the human brain. Some researchers say that the brain of the average person changes very little, especially in its ability to think and reason. All of us would probably be pleased to think that our brain power remains the same as we get older. That would be comforting, I guess, but it's not altogether true. But the truth sounds pretty good, too.

Recent research by psychologists, neuroscientists, and gerontologists is throwing a lot of doubt on earlier ideas that, when you get past middle age, your brain power goes away. A new breed of scientists (and gerontologists are a relatively new breed) is not always right about what they find out, but this time the scientists are probably a lot closer to the truth than earlier researchers who had a doomsday outlook about growing older.

Of course the human brain changes with age, but it changes a lot more between age 8 and 18 than it does between 48 and 68. And these changes can be good, especially if we are expecting them to be good. Most modern research is indicating that, from middle age to about age 75, the physical brain changes little in its ability to function. This research also suggests that our thinking and reasoning power does not change very much during that time either. Most of us, however, have been brainwashed to believe that our thinking and reasoning powers will begin to fade after 50 or so. This myth has resulted from bad research and those forces around us which would like us to think that we're fading in brain power as we get older.

Again, our attitude is the real key as to whether getting older will make us less capable of thinking clearly.

Many of us believe the myth that old age steals our ability to think. As a result, we indulge in a lot of self-pity and even harsh put-downs of ourselves, and that's wasted energy. We will not lose our ability to think, assuming, of course, that we have not had a stroke or experienced some physical condition that really does affect our brains. I am not saying that our intelligence doesn't change with age at all. Nevertheless, I do want us to use all the intelligence we have, to make the best use of what we have, and not to listen to things that don't apply to us. We are too smart to let a myth control our lives.

The Truth

God gave all of us the gift of intelligence. He didn't give us all the same amount to start with—but you already knew that. And even if you are among the unfortunate ones who have had a stroke or the like and if, because of this, you are not as sharp as you used to be, God expects you to maximize what you have.

Again, God didn't give each of us the same intellectual gift. Also, we are all undergoing changes, and we are not changing at the same pace or in the same way. But that doesn't matter. What does matter is the truth that most of us have a far greater gift of intellect than we have ever used. As we get older, it just may be necessary for us to use a little more of what we've got. So, if you're feeling sorry for yourself because you've heard that older people often lose the use of their minds, your thinking has to change.

Intellect or Wisdom?

I have been studying people for over forty years, and I think I've heard it all. At one time, for instance, psychologists were patronizing older people by saying, "Well, your brain doesn't work as well as it used to. But not to worry—your age has given you wisdom which is far more important than the smart-alecky brain power of the young."

Well, those psychologists were at least right about the wisdom. Solomon agrees. He said, "Wisdom is the principal thing" (Prov. 4:7). The psychologists and Solomon know that wisdom counts more than intelligence, and we older folk have been given the gift of wisdom. We've learned how to use our intellectual gifts wisely and how to make things happen with less physical power and less mental strain. Let me share an example from my own life.

About two years ago when I was working to clear a piece of land in the woods, I challenged the young man working with me to a contest. He was half my age, but I told him that I could cut down an eight-inch sapling faster than he could. I had my tree on the ground with about a dozen strokes of the ax. Despite his young strength, he whittled at his tree for a quarter of an hour. When he finally got it down, the stump looked like a beaver had done the work. Did I gloat? You bet I did!

You see, I had the wisdom, and he had the strength. Actually, I had the wisdom *and* the strength. Although this was primarily a physical contest, I had the wisdom I needed to use my strength effectively. Wisdom is gained through experience, and many times wisdom wins over both physical strength and pure intellectual power.

How Important Is Intellectual Power?

I think you will agree when I say that our society almost worships intellectual power. Every parent is anxious about whether or not their children have a high I.Q. (intelligence quotient). Teachers look at students' records to see how they scored on an intelligence test, how smart they are, and how quick they are to catch on. And people our age are concerned about their supposedly declining I.Q.

The Old Testament book of Proverbs shows that our modern society is not the only society concerned about wisdom and intelligence. Listen to what Solomon has to say about wisdom: "Get wisdom, get understanding: forget it not; neither decline from the words of my mouth. Forsake her not, and she shall preserve thee: love her, and she shall keep thee" (Prov. 4:5-6) and "For wisdom is better than rubies; and all the things that may be desired are not to be compared to it" (Prov. 8:11).

Wisdom was valued in Old Testament days. Is it valued as much today? Maybe we have come to place too much emphasis on intelligence and I.Q. scores, but we could never place too much emphasis on wisdom. For, you see, "The fear of the LORD is the beginning of knowledge" (Prov. 1:7) and "The fear of the LORD is the beginning of wisdom" (Prov. 9:10). Wisdom is a God-given and precious treasure that we acquire by walking through life with the Lord.

Wisdom is something you get, and you get it by knowing who the Lord is and by making Him Lord over your life. Only then can you and I receive wisdom and greater understanding. Wisdom and understanding come from your efforts, and keeping your wisdom and knowledge will also come from your efforts. You and I will, of course, give them up to some extent before God calls us home. Before we die, within the providence of God, you may have to give up some wisdom and knowledge as your body fails. But don't give them up out of laziness or because of a myth that says you should be less intelligent because you're growing old. You must ignore the voices of the world and continue to grow in wisdom and knowledge.

Again, intellectual power ultimately changes with age— that's God's plan. Time is in His hands, and He'll allow things to happen to you in His time, not yours. Don't take God's time into your own hands by voluntarily letting go of your intellectual power.

Changing Bodies and Changing Brains

Outdated research and human error have joined together to suggest that intellectual power declines because of physical aging. The fact is that nobody has yet proved that intellectual power actually declines with age, and it certainly doesn't decline to the degree that physical strength most often does. Although the brain is part of our physical body, that particular part of our body changes (slows its ability to function) at a much slower rate than the rest of our bodies.

Fluid vs. Crystallized Intelligence

Until the last ten years, researchers used the word *intelligence* to indicate what we mean when we say, "That child is really bright." We meant that the child (or any person, however old) catches on to new ideas quickly and easily. As a result, in the early years of psychology and gerontology, intelligence was thought of as the capacity to learn—and to learn quickly. I.Q. tests were constructed to measure people's capacity for learning and the quickness with which they grasped new information. Intelligence was seen as both the capacity to learn and an agility in learning.

People who are older lose some of the quickness, agility, and flexibility that they naturally had when they were younger. Researchers reasoned that the muscles in the brains lost agility and flexibility just as the muscles of the body did, and their I.Q. tests showed that to be the case. Since these tests measure capacity to learn, quickness, and agility, older test-takers showed a rather sharp decline beginning at about age 35.

But these tests reflected a very narrow view of intelligence.

The tests had nothing to do with the amount of knowledge a person might have. People may be totally ignorant and still have a high level of intelligence. That is, they might be able to catch on to new ideas quickly and easily. On the other hand, people may be very knowledgeable but not highly intelligent. With their hard work compensating for their lower intelligence, they may have gained a lot of information. But the tests focused only on the ability to learn and learn quickly.

Let's Get the Whole Story

As long as intelligence was defined as being quick to understand new information and as long as I.Q. tests were made to measure that rather than knowledge and understanding, it was hard for Bible scholars to find Scriptures relating to intelligence. As far as I have been able to determine, the word *intelligence* is not in the Bible.

About ten years ago, though, gerontologists started thinking about a different kind of intelligence. The idea of intelligence as brightness was labeled "fluid intelligence," and the new term "crystallized intelligence" was defined as "a usable and useful fund of knowledge together with attendant skills in using such knowledge." This new concept of intelligence focuses on how much knowledge we have and how well we use that information, reflecting a concept of intelligence quite different from the earlier one.

So psychologists made new tests designed to measure this newly-labeled kind of intelligence. And what do you know? This research supports an entirely different conclusion about the intelligence of us older folk. Using a test designed to measure crystallized intelligence, researchers found very little decline in I.Q. until about age 60, and many people showed no decline until age 74.[1]

By age 74, almost every person showed some decline, but the

amount of decline in many was negligible. The loss of intelligence seems to occur so slowly that most people are well into their 80s before it becomes a problem. For many people, the problems never became severe until shortly before death.

Now here is another important point. This crystallized intelligence can be studied by Bible scholars because it turns out to be approximately what Solomon called wisdom. And, according to Proverbs, wisdom is most often found in the seasoned, older person. Solomon himself, the wisest man who ever lived, often addresses his wise statements to "my son" (i.e., Prov. 6:20). With age comes wisdom.

Accomplishing Mental Tasks Quickly

Is there a real difference in the ability of young and old to do a complex task (like solving a difficult arithmetic problem) quickly? Yes, there is. Older persons have about as much ability to solve complex problems as do younger folk, but, in general, advancing age causes older folk to need a little more time to do so.

Researchers have dealt with so-called "speeded tasks" using subjects of all ages. The results confirm what most of us would expect. As a rule, increasing age causes the brain to function somewhat more slowly, but I don't think we ought to worry about this. Speed usually isn't important. Besides, slowing down is not the same as declining in ability. As a general rule, folk do slow down in their thinking. They can get the job done, but it takes a little longer. So what?

Actually, the speed at which we think might make a difference in the sort of work we do. Those jobs which require speed may be better off in the hands of younger folk, and that's sometimes a good reason to move over and let a younger person move in. But we don't have to take a backseat, and I won't allow you to limit yourself. If the change in your intellectual skills is a result of your age, I'm in favor of you realizing the fact. But if the change in your intellectual skills is brought about because you're listening to a lot of wrong information and your own voice telling you you've had it, I don't like it!

I've already passed 70, and I know that I've slowed down a little in my ability to handle highly complex problems—but I've only slowed down a little. For the most part, I only let the younger folk do what I didn't really care much about doing anyway. I've changed some in my intellectual skills, and I'm sure I'll change some more, but I wouldn't change places with anyone. Would you?

I hope you like being the person you are. You've got to if you are live according to God's plan, trusting that He made you the unique person you are and that, day by day, you are becoming more the person He wants you to be. Remember, too, that God gives us choices as we walk this path of life, and one of the most important choices we have is the attitude we have about things. That's important!

Intelligence and Physical Fitness

Can you maintain your intelligence by improving your physical fitness? Sure you can! After all, the human body is one unified system and not just a cluster of separate parts. It makes sense that the condition of our heart, lungs, muscles, and blood affects our brain power.

So if you want to maintain your physical fitness, what can you do? Well, several things, of course. Exercising regularly and eating right are two important things. One of the great side effects is that keeping physically fit helps your I.Q. remain relatively stable.

In a study done in 1980, people scored better on some I.Q. tests after doing physical exercises than they did before the exercises.[2] (I guess that the exercises at the very least sent more blood to the brain, but any toning of the body is going to have a helpful effect on the brain. Remember, though, that moderation is a watchword in all things.) Studies also show that—all other things being equal—inactive, sedentary people experience the greatest decline in intelligence.[3]

But there is another kind of exercise that can help keep your mind sharp, and that's mental exercise. Reading books, taking classes, solving puzzles, and working math problems are all mental exercises. Word games, conversations with smart people, informative television shows, and listening to your minister will also provide you with a mental workout.[4] There are thousands of mental exercises. Will exercises like these keep your intellectual juices going? Absolutely!

Researchers have seen that mental activity helps intellectual performance. The more of these intellectual exercises you do, the longer you will maintain your brain power. In other words, we need to "use it or lose it." Most of us retire from jobs, vocations, and professions, but we should not retire our minds. People who don't retire mentally will never grow old at heart.

End-of-Chapter Questions

What myths about mental capacity had you heard and perhaps even believed? How has your experience refuted those myths?

In your own words, how are wisdom and intelligence different? Which do you value more? Why?

When has your wisdom helped you win over physical strength or intellectual power? Or when have you seen someone else's wisdom help him or her succeed at something?

Look again at the list of mental exercises in the second to the last paragraph. Are you getting your minimum daily requirement of mental stimulation? Choose one or two of these activities many of which are within easy reach to tackle before the day ends.

What have you always wanted to learn more about? A certain person? A specific time in history? A foreign language? A higher level of math? The Bible? Architecture? Music? Art? The possibilities for learning are endless. Choose a topic and head to your local library! What's to stop you?

CHAPTER 12

How Is Your Memory?

"Remember the days of old, consider the years of many generations . . ."—Deuteronomy 32:7

One of the most upsetting tales you hear about getting old is that your memory fades away. Well, it's true to a degree, but probably not like you've been led to think. Our memory does decline with age, but it's often not anything to worry about. To hear some people tell it, though, dramatic memory loss happens to everyone without fail. If that's so, there must be at least a few exceptions. I myself am one. How about you?

Myths and wild tales are seldom recognized for what they are. Why? Mostly because there is just enough truth in the stories to keep them going. Some people do have poorer memories as they grow older. The really sad part is that so many of us, hearing that we are supposed to become forgetful, really do become forgetful. Are you letting other people decide for you that you are losing your memory? I hope not.

Remembering Is Hard Work

Having a good active memory means that you must put forth effort—sometimes a lot of effort. And think about it. Hasn't it always been that way? Even for youngsters, remembering is work, but they know intuitively how important it is and automatically work at it. Many folk our age get lazy about remembering things like names and telephone numbers. They simply don't make any effort to remember, saying, "I'm getting older, you know. I'm not supposed to have a good memory." And sure enough, they don't. They don't have to remember things in order to make a living like the young businessman does, so they don't work at it.

Willing to Work

You and only you can determine whether or not you have a good memory or a poor one. If you want to take the easy way out and have people feel sorry for you, if you want to give up your job, or if you want to put things off on your children that you could do better yourself, you can choose to have a poor memory. Most people, including your children, will not contradict you when you tell them your memory is failing. First of all, you will be letting your behavior support your assertion. And, second, they have been snowed by the same tales that you've been snowed by.

But you don't have to go along with the idea that failing memory is a burden all older people have to bear. The fact is that you can improve your memory at almost any age, and people of any age who believe this fact can develop better memories than they had when they were 20. Try this: Decide that you are going to remember all the important telephone numbers you have to deal with. Then work at it.

- The first three numbers of any phone number are always easy. You can usually associate them with certain parts of the city. In our town, the 776 numbers are in a pretty high-class part of town while the 799 numbers are in a small

adjoining town and a large rural area. Learn the neighbor-
hoods served by each prefix in your area.

- Now concentrate on the last four numbers. Try to picture
them in your mind. Repeat them over and over again. Are
any of the last four numbers the same as the first three? Say
the entire number aloud a time or two.

- After you have committed several numbers to memory, go
the phone and call these numbers. Call all of the numbers
you want to remember, even if you have to make up excuses
for calling people.

Let's Be Honest

You're probably saying, "Doesn't that man know about Alzheimer's disease?" I certainly do, and that disease is a scary
possibility for older folk. While strokes, Alzheimer's, and
other diseases which affect one's memory are all frighteningly
real, the worst of it is that a lot of elderly folk are panicking
unnecessarily. "Could this be happening to me?" they ask. And
then they start looking for signs that their memory is fading
and conclude that they have contracted a serious disease.

Does that sound like you? Then look at the percentages.
Less than five percent of the population dies from so-called catastrophic diseases. So maybe all this hype about Alzheimer's is
something you should practice forgetting instead of reminding
yourself to remember! Too many of us are worried about something that will probably never happen to us . . . .

A friend of mine who is over 65 did a strange thing the other
day. She unplugged her iron and put it in her refrigerator. After
she realized what she'd done, she really panicked. She was ter-
rified that this was the first sign of Alzheimer's. When we
talked about it, I asked her to recall something really embar-
rassing she had done in earlier years. She remembered an incident from her freshman year in college. The building where

classes were held had three stories, and each floor looked pretty much like the other two. Her English class was on the third floor. One day when my friend was delayed getting back from lunch, she rushed up to the second floor. Being a little late, she entered the room with her head down and slipped quietly into what she thought was her assigned seat. She soon she realized she was listening to a chemistry lecture. She sat paralyzed for the entire hour and then slipped out unnoticed.

I hope the point of this story is clear. You and I can do some really silly things when we're 65, but they are often a poor match for the silly things we did when we were 18. But the myth that we will lose our memory is out to get us, and the media blitz on Alzheimer's doesn't help either. Added to that, some of your friends and loved ones have had strokes or are being placed in nursing homes with problems labeled Alzheimer's whether or not that diagnosis is correct. I hope the facts here help counter the myth and calm your fears.

What a Brain We Have

The workings of the human neurological system are truly unbelievable, existing as they do only because of our great Creator's infinite knowledge and skilled craftsmanship. How can it be even remotely possible to remember sixty-five years later something that happened to you when you were five years old? Well, it happens because the Lord God created man and woman as superior creatures, and when He was finished, He "saw everything that he had made, and, behold, *it was very good*" (Gen. 1:31, emphasis mine).

The Human Body: A Miracle of Creation

The human body has offered a pattern for many inventions in our age of technology. The invention of the camera would have been impossible if the inventor had had no knowledge of the human eye, and computers are described as miniature human brains. The power of the computer to store and then recover information at the touch of a button is possible only because the human brain first conceived the computer and then built the computer after the model of the human brain. Although extremely useful as a time-saver and a work-saver, the computer is, of course, far inferior to the brain that conceived it and then fashioned it out of silicon and plastic.

The Human Brain: Super Miracle

The Bible speaks of the heart as the seat of righteousness, in a general way, as the seat of the emotions, and, in some senses, as the seat of motivation and wisdom. But the Scripture has little to say about the brain as an instrument of thinking or remembering. God inspired the writers of Scripture to communicate what they understood about their bodies. God, however, understands completely how the human brain and the heart function. He understands memory far better than all of today's scientists and doctors, and He is even now releasing His own understanding through the work of modern researchers.

Memory is possible because of what God did on the sixth day when He created the intricate human brain. We know with reasonable certainty that the brain is the seat of memory. Medical researchers and surgeons know that, when certain brain centers are destroyed, memory is erased. The brain is our memory bank: everything we ever knew is stored there, to be retrieved at our command.

The human brain is made up of over ten billion cells. These cells are grouped together to form lobes, and each lobe has a specific task. One lobe is responsible for seeing, another for hearing, and still another for tasting and smelling. Other parts of the brain are memory banks where everything we've ever ex-

112

perienced is stored. Brain surgeons can stimulate certain parts of your brain when you are in surgery, and, right there on the operating table, you will sing the songs your mother used to sing to you at bedtime. All of your experiences are stored in your brain. Some of them you can get out (retrieve) very easily; others you can't remember at all.

How Memories Get into Your Brain

Memories get into your brain through your own efforts. You remember telephone numbers because you make an effort to learn them. Learning can be done very deliberately or very casually. If you learn something only casually, however, the impact (encoding) on your brain cells is not very strong, and that means you will have trouble remembering (retrieving) that piece of information. You can't remember very well what you didn't learn well, and you can remember more easily those things which you learned really well.

Helping Memory Along

Learning a telephone number really well is likely to occur if you think you need that number. You learn your children's telephone numbers well because you know you are going to need them. More than that, you likely use the numbers regularly. Even if you don't call your children very often, you probably repeat those numbers to yourself several times a day because you really want to remember them. Perhaps a dozen times a day you think, "Maybe I ought to call Susie," and whether or not you call her, you rehearse the number to be sure you remember it. You surely have rehearsed your physician's number, the number of an ambulance service, or your police department's number—and certainly 911!

What I am getting at is that your memory depends less on

your age than it does on the quality of your learning. People blame their weakening memory on age, but it isn't age. It's just that as you and I get older, some of us get indifferent or a little lazy about learning things really well, and we don't rehearse the pieces of information. Older people who realize this tendency make up their minds to learn things well, and they rehearse those things they think they may need to remember. So the problem isn't age; most of the time it's our level of motivation that's at fault.

You may be saying, "Who wants or even needs to do that much remembering anyway?" It's your choice, but don't get down on yourself and say you can't remember because you are getting too old. That's a cop-out, but you can cop out if you want to. That is your privilege. But don't give up a job, claiming your failing memory as the reason, when that really isn't the case. You may have a dozen good reasons for quitting work, and that's fine. Maybe you want to smell the roses instead of work. Again, fine. Just keep it straight why you are doing what you're doing. Your age is probably not a factor in your ability to remember.

Short-term and Long-term Memory

I'm sure you've heard people say that they can remember things that happened a long time ago better than things that happened yesterday or last week. That's understandable because those things that happened long ago were probably very important to you and were impacted on your brain very powerfully. Added to that, you have probably been remembering those things over and over, sharing stories about your childhood years with friends, and laughing with brothers and sisters about the crazy things you used to do when you were kids. You have been rehearsing those memories for years—perhaps even spicing up the events of your childhood! The things you did last week, however, probably weren't that exciting, and you probably haven't rehearsed them by telling others about them.

One more point about short-term memory. When people get really old (and it varies from one person to another), they may have a loss of short-term memory. Understand, though, that short-term memory, as the psychologists and brain specialists use the term, is not for remembering what happened yesterday or last week. Actually, short-term memory is really short—like thirty seconds. For some reason, very old persons can't store memories quickly, and things that don't get stored can't be remembered.

This type of problem with short-term memory is the reason why some very old people shouldn't drive. When these folk are entering the street and cars are approaching from both directions, they have problems. They look to the right and see cars coming, and then they look to the left and see a delivery truck coming. All the while, they are desperately trying to get out into the stream of traffic. They don't have time to store the information about the delivery truck because they know they've got to quickly look back to the right to see if all the other cars have passed and no one else is coming. When they see the way clear on the right, they pull out straight into the path of the delivery truck and get hit. Did their short-term memory of the delivery truck fail them? What probably happened was that the information about the delivery truck was never stored in the brain. If it wasn't stored, how could they remember it?

We know that, at some point, the learning-storing process gets slowed down. It may start slowing down a little at a time long before the slowness becomes significant enough to affect our life. But we do have to face the fact that, sooner or later, our bodies are going to decline. And sooner or later we elderly people will need to consider our memory as well as our eyesight when we choose our activities.

Let's Face It

There will come a time when your memory will not be as good as it was twenty years ago or as it is now. True, you can prolong serious decline in your memory by working at remembering things, but sooner or later you will probably decide that the reward is not worth the struggle. So be it. Maybe the happiest days of your life will come after that. After all, someday we will be with the God who made us. Then whatever we have lost will be restored.

End-of-Chapter Questions

What is the first thing you remember memorizing as a child? How did you feel about your accomplishment? How hard did you have to work?

How many phone numbers have you memorized according to my suggestions? See the ol' memory still works!

Think of a silly thing you did recently. Compare it to a slip of your memory or an unthinking action from 30, 40, or even 50 years ago. Have a good laugh, realizing that you're human and not necessarily losing your memory!

What Scripture passages have you committed to memory through the years? Is it time to brush up on some of those?

Choose from the Bible a passage of Scripture which you have never before memorized. It doesn't have to be long to be a good workout for your memory!

CHAPTER 13

Love of Family

"I will arise and go to my father."—Luke 15:18

With His story about the Prodigal Son, Jesus teaches us how valuable our relationship to our heavenly Father is. Each one of us is a prodigal son or daughter whose heavenly Father grants us freedom, waits for our return, and celebrates our reunion with Him. That generous love of the Father is the kind of love we should ideally find in our family. And when we have grown up with that kind of love, those ties of love that bind us together with our family often become more important as we age.

The Origin of Family

Family bonds reflect the love God has for His own Son. He extends that love to believers, and when we receive that love, we become His family on earth. The love of our earthly family is to reflect this divine love, but family bonds are severely strained for most of us. Many families do remain strongly bonded, but that isn't always the case. The calls to find one's personal identity, gain one's goal in the business world, and climb the ladder of affluence—these and various other factors cause people to work less on building family ties during their young adult and child-rearing years.

As we age, we may continue to find causes for this distance within our family. However, most of us feel the need to return to the closeness which only family members can feel for each other. We yearn most strongly to be close to our sons, daughters, grandchildren, fathers, and mothers, more than to our sisters and brothers.

The increase in life expectancy has had a dramatic impact on how families relate. These additional years mean additional stress especially on the relationship between parents and children. Sadly, it is almost as if parents—living, on average, to 76—are living too long, thereby creating stress that otherwise would not arise. But other changes in culture and society have also had a dramatic impact on family life. Rising divorce rates, teenage pregnancies, and drug addiction are other stressful realities affecting today's families.

The Extended Family and the Nuclear Family

There was a time when persons of several generations lived under the same roof. This was called the extended family. Elderly people were deeply cherished and more respected than they are today. They lived at home and found a rich identity as they shared love and work with younger generations. Today's modern family is, most often, the nuclear family: husband, wife, and a child or two. In the nuclear family, there is no place for the elderly. The fact that both spouses work leaves no one to take care of either the young or the elderly. Although a majority of widows live with their daughters and a majority of the elderly continue to sustain themselves in their own homes, there is an increasing need for institutional care of the elderly as well as day-care for children.

118

Family Relationships: Boon or Curse to the Elderly?

We who are 50-plus are sometimes acting as parents to our own parents at the same time that we have children and often grandchildren of our own. We are known as the "sandwich generation" because we are sandwiched between at least two generations who need us desperately.

Stress Mounts with Increasing Life Expectancy

Not very long ago, being 50 gave people the right and privilege of fewer responsibilities and the freedom to let younger folk shoulder most of the family responsibilities and consequent stress. But today we 50-plus people have one generation above us (our mothers and fathers) and possibly even another (our grandparents), and most of us have at least two generations below us. As a result, few of us are relieved of family responsibility or stress. As a matter of fact, our stress level is likely to rise.

Many people in the Deep South, however, still regard age 50 as a turning point. The family patriarch calls his children together to announce a changing of the guard. One young man, an advisee of mine at Baylor who wanted to go on to graduate school, came in to see me one day. His wealthy family had large farm holdings in western Texas, and they virtually owned a small town there. The family owned the bank, the grocery store, the hardware store—almost everything.

But Dad had turned 50, and not only did he tell my advisee that he was turning the family businesses over to him, but he also told his son that it was the young man's duty to come home and take charge. The young man was in love with a lovely girl at Baylor, hated farm life, and knew he would lose the girl if he went back to manage the family holdings. The outcome? He left the family. Happily, an older sister was delighted to take over the family business, but the young man's anguish was terrible.

In a way, I guess, we have to admire this wealthy farmer who chose to follow the family tradition of turning everything over to his son. Most of us, whose heritages do not embrace this notion, have continued to be involved in the family and so continued to feel the stress that can come with major responsibility. Stress can be especially high when those of us who are 70 have frail parents in their 90s who require much from us, too. Besides having responsibilities to older generations, people who are 50-plus are much closer to the heartbreaking problems of their children and grandchildren, and that is an additional source of stress.

A Case in Point

Consider Sally who, at 75, is a healthy and hearty widow. Her husband, Carl, died five years ago, and Sally's parents have both passed on to be with the Lord. Sally, however, is the chief caretaker of her 92-year-old mother-in-law, who lived with Sally and Carl until Carl died. Her mother-in-law accepted quite ungraciously her move into a nursing home. She never really understood why Sally couldn't care for her at home, and she is filled with rancor for having been abandoned. Sally visits Carl's mother at least three times a week, taking her special things to eat and seeing that she is not too lonely. Sally feels these are the Christian things to do, and she is right.

Carl and Sally had three children of their own and enjoyed a good life of considerable affluence. Carl left Sally well-fixed with ample savings and a nice income. It's too bad that Sally couldn't have kept her financial status a secret from at least two of her children.

Daughter Carole, now 50, has a recently-married daughter attending the university and a son in medical school. Sally's son, James Edward, has a good dental practice but is an alcoholic. Carole and James Edward live in the same city as Sally. Maxwell, the third child, has moved to another city, gained his independence, and is a joy to Sally when she sees him—likely only once a year. Sally has seven grandchildren, two of whom are married, and no great grandchildren yet.

Financial Pressures of the Young-Old

Sally's children obtained good educations before Carl passed away, so one would expect all three to be financially independent. Such is not the case for either Carole or James Edward.

James Edward, although ostensibly a successful professional, has been in financial trouble since his marriage. James Edward's wife spends more on clothes in a month than Sally allows herself in a year. Both of James Edward's sons drive expensive sports cars, and James Edward is no penny-pincher either. Sally has rescued James Edward from one financial debacle after another. Twice in the last month, Sally has had to bail him out of jail for driving while intoxicated. His dear wife simply calls Sally and tells her that her son is in jail again.

Carole has a near-derelict husband and three very expensive children. She has tapped Sally's till time and time again. The latest drain on the family fortune (controlled by Sally, yet out of control) was the granddaughter's very extravagant wedding, the cost of which by some weird twist fell on Sally's dwindling pocketbook. Sally is watching her funds drain away as she pays the nursing home costs for Carl's mother, maintains her own household, and picks up the financial slack for James Edward and Carole. Unless she calls a halt to the pattern, she will be shouldering the financial responsibility for a new set of great-grandchildren. Sally feels guilty that she is quietly glad Maxwell had the good judgment to move to another city.

And Sally is getting worried. No amount of money could

survive the demands currently being made on her finances. How long will there be enough for her mother-in-law's care? Will there be anything left for Sally? We've all heard about cases like this where the generous but not very assertive money-giver winds up with nothing and has to live on Medicaid. What can and should Sally do? That's a tough question, and I'm not sure any of us could do any better than she is doing. Ideally and logically, she should call the family together and explain why she must withdraw financial support. But nine chances out of ten, if she does that, she'll be sorry. It may cost her dearly in terms of her family relationships.

Maybe Sally should turn to the Lord with her problems, asking Him to guide her and enable her to be strong and trusting Him to care for James Edward and Carole. With His presence, perhaps her children would understand and accept the change if and when Sally withdraws financial support. God can be Sally's comfort and hope. Only He can see her through this morass.

Inheritances in a Time of Aging

All three of Sally's children are on the verge of becoming senior citizens, yet two of them are still dependent on Sally for substantial financial help. Is this right? If it isn't, then who is wrong? Sadly, good-hearted Sally is wrong and has been for many years.

But family situations like this are difficult. What elderly person can say no to an adult child who has fallen on bad times, regardless of whose fault it is? Not many of us can. Much of the time, the adult children are issuing veiled commands; their requests for financial assistance suggest that we owe it to them. Some will actually say, "Mother and Daddy, why don't you go ahead and give me my inheritance now while I can still enjoy it?"

The fact is that adult children should forget about—or at least never count on—an inheritance, and it is up to us, their parents, to see that they understand this. The elderly may cherish the idea of leaving the children a nest egg, but the years of our life have become too many and medical costs have become too high to guarantee inheritances for our children.

We have worked for fifty years or more, provided well for our children's education and vocational opportunities, and offered them our emotional support. Furthermore, we should not indulge our children by enabling them to live better than we ourselves do. That can and does happen when we are foolish enough to want a certain standard of living for them and they are foolish enough to accept our unwise generosity.

Again, we are the sandwiched generation. Some of us may have received substantial inheritances ourselves, but that practice seems to be changing. At the end of the twentieth century, it seems to me that the hard-working elderly have spoiled their adult children, spending on them whatever inheritance they might have—rightfully or wrongfully—expected. We did the spoiling; maybe we deserve what we are now getting from our adult children.

Some Adult Children Are Gems

The picture I have painted is certainly not the only one out there. Many adult children are lovingly committed to their elderly fathers and mothers. And, of course, some adult children deserve many stars in their heavenly crowns because of their unselfish dedication to Mom, Dad, and other elderly family members. Those of us who visit or work at nursing homes these days see this dedication quite often. But, in the main, adult children are not always caring for their parents with any sense of love or joy.

Are adult children right when they place themselves and

their young families first? Yes, of course, they are. Their own family is their first priority. Are they right to withdraw moral, financial, and emotional support from aging mothers and fathers? No, they definitely are not. That is neither a biblical nor a loving response. But aren't our adult children members of a sandwiched generation, too? Certainly they are. Some are sandwiched between us, their fathers and mothers, and their own children and grandchildren. So what can we say about these sandwiched generations?

A Return to Love

A large part of the overriding problem is that we have yielded ourselves to stress and worry and have lost sight of the principle of love and that is easy to do . . . .

Consider Paula and Dan. They are in their early 50s, and their three children are in their mid- to late 30s. The oldest of their five teenage grandchildren is entering the university this fall, and the other four are looking forward to university educations and glorious futures beyond. Paula and Dan received bounteous educations and generous financial help from their parents. Do they owe the same to their children? They certainly feel that they do. Unfortunately there is not that much money, and there are many demands on the money which is available.

Three parents remain. Paula's father, who was quite well-to-do, passed on a few years ago, leaving his sizable estate to Paula's mother who, at 69, is its fierce guardian. Paula's mother is not the giving type, but Paula feels that her mother should see the problems which she and Dan are facing. Even a few hundred dollars would help ease the pressure. Sure, she and Dan have a fine home and three cars, but nothing is really paid for. Besides, Dan's business interests demand an affluent lifestyle.

In contrast to Paula's folks, Dan's parents never had much of this world's goods. In their late 70s, they are fine people, but they didn't think at all in terms of creating wealth or saving for retirement. Now they are both sick, but they still live in the family home which is deteriorating along with their health and financial reserves. Both should be in a nursing home, but they refuse to sell the old house, get on Medicaid, and enter a home. It would be such a relief to Dan if they would.

In spite of his bad heart, Dan is pushing himself to the breaking point to see that his parents are well cared for, and Paula, a sincere and loving Christian, does all she can to help. She fixes meals constantly and regularly takes both Dan's parents to the doctor. Also, with her children's help, Paula gets these dear people to their church at least twice a week.

And Paula worries about Dan's heart problem. He had a triple bypass a year ago, and the doctor recommends rest and no stress. "Oh, Mother," she thinks fervently as she sees those university costs coming, "can't you kill the fatted calf right now and give us a little help?"

Can We Avoid These Dilemmas?

The situations Sally and Paula find themselves in show the complications that can arise when people live longer than they used to. We can't expect to untangle these complex situations without God's love and presence among us.

But not everyone's heart is full of God's love. The children's bills may be piling up while their seemingly senile young-old and old-old relatives hold on to their money. People 50-plus struggle with health and finances. People of 70-plus grieve over what seems to them neglect and health problems. Indeed, gross neglect is evident in nursing homes, and we all shudder when the media appropriately focuses on the horrible treatment of the frail elderly. Grasping manipulators of human misery appall us with their crass commercialism. They bilk the elderly in ways that are anything but Christian. Even some of our own actions and words when we're dealing with our family members—especially the older generations—can sometimes be quite unchristian.

God, however, can provide enough love to go around. God is not dead; He is not absent from these difficult situations. He may, however, be testing us, and we must indeed pray for guidance and relief. We must also rest in His promise that He never leaves or forsakes us, even though our lives are fraught with vexations (Josh. 1:5).

The Line of First Defense

Not a single one of us has been able to escape the vexations of growing old and the pressures of caring for aging people, both younger and older than us. Family bonds can undoubtedly be strained to the breaking point, and we can always find fault with the seeming selfishness of people whom we think could help us out if they only cared enough.

We should, however, be guardians of our own Christian virtue rather than detractors of those who seem not to measure up, those who seem neglectful, grasping, and selfish. God will judge. We cannot help making judgments, but our judgments may be very inaccurate. We walk poorly enough in our own shoes, and we'd undoubtedly do worse in the shoes of others. Each of us has our own vexations, and each of us—with God's help—must shoulder our load.

Foresight Is Better Than Hindsight

Those of us who are 50-plus or even 70-plus may have waited too long to completely revise our ways of seeing and doing things. Many of us would have benefited from planning ahead for our aging many years ago. But young people—and we were probably no exception—typically cannot face growing old and cannot easily be enticed into thinking so far ahead.

No matter what our age, we can still gain new insights and change unhealthy patterns of behavior. True, every case—with its special set of pressures and stresses—is unique. Trying to make general comments could be very hazardous. Still, at the risk of being too general, let me offer the following:

On Family Love, Loyalty, and Unity

The teachings of Christ as well as teachings from the Jewish tradition emphasize filial love, obligation, and unity. The Bible's references to the family of God, human brotherhood in Christ, the sanctity of marriage, and the importance of parent-child bonding teach us that relationships with family members are different from associations with persons of no blood relation. The Christian is called upon to honor father and mother. Wives and husbands, although having no common bloodlines, are urged to give each to the other the highest honor and esteem—forsaking all others.

On Family Finance

As long as possible, financial affairs should be handled by both spouses together and then by the one remaining spouse. You can share your financial resources with others, but I suggest that a measure of candid nondisclosure surround your financial affairs as long as you or your spouse is capable of money management.

You may want to give your children and other loved ones financial assistance. I encourage you to offer this assistance in the form of loans. Of course, many parents can and do make free-will gifts to their children, but these gifts should be shared wisely.

Loans to family members should be clearly defined as such, but you should never make a loan you can not afford to consider a gift. Family members, even with due consideration to the principles of filial love, are often notorious non-payers of loans they receive from other family members.

Let me also encourage you to depend on reputable professionals for financial advice on investments, wills, trusts, etc. There usually comes a time, however, when children must be made privy to their parents' financial affairs. When this occurs, all children should be involved even though one may be given a stronger leadership role.

On Inheritances

Inheritances and the dispersal of so-called inheritances before death is a very personal matter. Let me offer some general warnings and basic principles:

1. The state of the economy, the possibility of catastrophic illnesses, the future needs of our mate, and various unpredictable events including the length of our life make it impossible to know how much money will be enough to live on. Except in cases of disabled, mentally retarded, or other types of continuously dependent children, it seems wise not to divide inheritances before the death of both spouses. To do so might endanger your own financial security as well as prevent adult children from establishing their own solid careers and developing their own financial resources.

2. The most meaningful gift a parent can give a child is self-confidence, and self-confidence does not come from dependence. In these days, however, young adults training to be professionals may need financial help a number of years after they reach age 18. Parents who can afford to

might continue to support their children's efforts to reach their potential and fulfill their dreams.

3. Inheritances should be thought of as gifts of love, not as obligations.

4. When one spouse dies, the remaining one should divide that spouse's wealth among the children only if there is sure to be a surplus beyond his/her possible needs.

5. As long as both spouses are active and alert, each should will all properties and wealth to the other, making specific arrangements for unexpected disability or demise. Questions surrounding inheritance taxes must also be considered.

On Living Arrangements

Don't let yourself be pressured into giving up your home or other cherished properties. The best place for older people is in our home where we can manage our own affairs. Obviously, this scenario is sometimes unreasonable or impractical, and other arrangements must be made.

Since expectations determine attitudes, older folk would do well to choose self-management and expect to succeed at it. Given that necessity alters circumstances, adult children should support their parents' choice to remain as functioning husbands and wives and self-managing home owners as long as possible.

Entrepreneurs are providing an increasing number of living arrangements for elderly citizens who have money or government support. While I'm not going to review the variety of living arrangements available, I would like to offer three suggestions:

1. Any and every living arrangement offered for the elderly is based on the economic welfare of someone other than

the elderly person who pays. If there are exceptions, this author isn't aware of them.

2. Regardless of the attractive features presented by entrepreneurs, that attractiveness is not guaranteed to be permanent. If the food is excellent, it may soon not be so excellent. If the nursing care is adequate, it may vary from tolerable to terrible. There is no free lunch, and lunches you pay for are often not as palatable as they appear.

3. Adult children (at whatever age) should not depend on the constancy of any living arrangement made by their parents, by the adult children themselves, or by any combination of interested parties. Constant vigilance is the only way to insure the adequacy of an older person's living arrangements.

Love of family can be difficult and complicated as we grow older. Finances and living arrangements are two sticking points which each of us must deal with. My prayer is that God will bless you—and the generations before and after you—with a sense of His very real and very abundant love. May His love help you work through the touchy family matters that we all encounter.

End-of-Chapter Questions

How have you experienced changing family patterns? Compare the people in your parents' families to those in the home you grew up in and the home of one of your children. What were the benefits and drawbacks of the three different arrangements?

What changings of the guard have you seen in your family? What good things resulted?

What lessons can be learned from Sally's or Paula's situation? Do any of those lessons apply to your current situation?

What practical suggestions on family finances, inheritances, and living arrangements do you find most helpful? Which one can you act on now?

How can you be a channel of God's love in your current family situation? Do you need to extend forgiveness? Do you need to apologize? Do you need to reevaluate your expectations? Pray that God will fill you with His love and enable you to do what you need to do.

CHAPTER 14

Should You
Ever Retire?

❧

"Take my yoke upon you, and learn of me; for I am meek and lowly in heart: and ye shall find rest unto your souls."—Matthew 11:29

❧

Every one of us who is working at a regular job to earn a living knows that one day we'll retire. For the most part, retirement benefits are built into every job in industrial and corporate America, and most of us look forward to the day when we will not have to work. There are, however, serious questions about the benefits of retiring just because we are free to do so. Besides, as far as the Lord's work is concerned, we need not ever retire until a very few days before we meet the Lord face to face.

Retirement Planning

The choice of vocation is an important decision, and the variety of opportunities is vast. When we made our choices, we were undoubtedly urged to give a lot of thought to what we wanted to do and how we would prepare for that career. A prime consideration in choosing a vocation was whether we'd enjoy what we'd be doing and, ideally, whether we felt called by God to do it.

Those of us who are fortunate have jobs we basically enjoy, but liking one's work is a relative thing. Every job means work,

132

and any work has its difficult or burdensome elements. Jobs, no matter how much we may like them, make demands on us, intrude on our lives, and require large blocks of our time and much of our energy. Even when we're working hard at our career, though, we need to spend some time and energy planning for retirement.

Approaching Retirement

People usually approach retirement with eager anticipation, counting off the years and months until they can "hang it up." Many of us make ambitious and detailed plans about what we'll do during our retirement years. We dream about how we'll spend our time doing just what we've always wanted to do. And most of us usually have made careful investments and built up financial reserves to see us through our retirement years.

How much we anticipate retirement depends greatly on how much we liked our jobs. It also varies according to the type work we do. The person who has spent many years in back-breaking physical labor needs to give his body a break and count the days until he doesn't have to push his body any longer. Workers whose job entails the constant pressure of serving the public or dealing with constant noise and confusion feel the need to give their nerves a break. They need to get away from the stress.

Professionals—especially when they're people pleasers—often work under great amounts of stress. Some professionals look forward to retirement because their mind or hands have become unsteady, too unsteady to put other lives at risk. In medical careers, for instance, human lives depend on professional expertise and careful judgments. Such work generates a special kind of stress.

For every one of us, retiring from work will mean getting out from under physical, emotional, or managerial stress. Right now, we yearn for that freedom. We long for the perpetual weekend—or at least we think we do.

Getting Involved in Something New

When we retire, most of us are just as anxious to get involved in something new as we are to get out of the old. We want (or think we want) to garden, to fish, to play golf, or to travel. Most of us want to get away from some things and get involved in other things.

We are all smart enough to know that the play we anticipate could become tiresome just as the work we do becomes tiresome. So we must plan for variety. Many people plan well and experience long retirements of blissful activity combined with the right amount of "just doing nothing."

The Long Years of Retirement

Most of us fail to recognize how long retirement can last. Since there can be a lot of years, it is usually a mistake to expect some kind of euphoric retirement that will last for the thirty or more remaining years of our life. We often find ourselves needing to retire from our retirements. To the chagrin of many of my friends, they have found retirement to be a bore.

As we experience the added years of our life, many of us are seeing that a truly successful retirement consists more of changing jobs than of leaving a job behind. Some of my friends can truly enjoy doing nothing gainful for thirty or more years. Maybe they are the lucky ones, and certainly they are entitled to that carefree option of traveling, puttering, and doing nothing. But that option is not for everyone.

The Two People Involved in Retirement

One thing that must be considered in retirement is the compatibility of you and your spouse. Do your ideas and dreams for retirement match? It is a fact that retirement can put greater strain on a marriage than the routine of the working days ever did!

Nonworking spouses face as great—if not a greater—adjustment to the retirement of the worker than the worker himself does. Let me tell you about two of my friends who retired at 65. Having decided to stay with my profession until age 70, I eagerly watched them. I thought Ruth and I could learn a lot from their experiences.

Louie and Evelyn Summers approached retirement gleefully. Louie was an executive in a large company. He had over five hundred employees under his direct supervision, and almost all five hundred attended his retirement dinner. Louie was showered with praise for a job well done and assured, with much backslapping, that "we'll keep in touch, buddy." The couple bought an attractive bungalow on a lake and began their retirement. I saw Louie a few days ago some two years after the big dinner. As I prepared for my own job exodus, I asked him how retirement was treating him.

"We're having a ball, Les," he said. "We pretty much have a routine. One day we fish, one day a week we play golf, and in between we just do what we want to do. We make short trips to places we enjoy, eat at favorite restaurants, and spend time with favorite friends. We are very active in church, and we're having a ball."

I believe Louie was telling me just the way it was. "Oh yes, Les," he said, "you remember those five hundred people who said they'd stay in touch? Well, in two years we haven't seen a single one of them. We do have a lot of church friends, and it's great to see you, buddy. Why don't you go on and hang it up? Don't worry—retirement is great!"

I believed Louie, but I couldn't help wondering just how long all his happiness could last. I know that people often cover up their retirement woes. They're supposed to be happy, so they put on happy faces. Others, like Stewart and Dorothy Jumper, openly talk about the disappointments and miseries of retirement.

Stewart had been a corporate attorney and Dorothy a legal secretary. They agreed to retire at the same time although both could have continued working a little longer.

"We're miserable," Dorothy volunteered. "Stewart is like a caged tiger, and so am I. He's driving me nuts being around the house all the time. He was supposed to plant a big garden. Take a good look at his fine crop of weeds! He played more golf when he was working than he does now—and he enjoys it a lot less. As for me, I think I'm going bananas."

People experience quite a letdown when they find that they miss the old job and their former associates and they look ahead to the seemingly meaningless years which stretch before them. One wife of a retired golfing buddy told me, "For a lot of years, we had teenagers to entertain for three whole months during summer vacations. I felt like I'd go crazy before they got back in school in the fall. I always celebrated that glorious event for weeks. Well, You-Know-Who is worse than six teenagers rolled into one—and his vacation is going to last forever! I'd give anything to get him off my back." Of course, she was half-kidding—but only half.

Retirement: A Long-term Goal

Most of us simply cannot envision a thirty-year or even a twenty-year retirement, so we make plans as if retirement were going to last only a few years. When we began our marriages, though, we did so knowing that our lives for the next thirty years or so would be lived out in a logical pattern: the adaptation phase, the child-bearing stage, the child-rearing stage, formal schooling, the teenage years, college days, and then the empty nest. We were prepared for the stages of life between marriage and age 50.

We don't, however, tend to think of retirement in stages, and we don't plan retirement very specifically. We have only a general idea of what we're going to do, and we think about retirement as if it is one span of time.

The Stages of Long-term Retirement

As a psychologist for thirty years, I have watched a variety of people retire, including my own parents, the parents of my friends, and my clients. Let me share two anecdotes.

Alice and Tom Huston retired at 62 because Social Security benefits encouraged retirement at this early age. Both of them had starry-eyed expectations about traveling and taking life easy—and that was about twenty-five years ago. Alice, now 85, is in a nursing home with multiple medical problems including a recently-acquired broken hip. In her most lucid moments Alice talks a lot about Tom and the wonderful life they had together.

In reality, the Hustons' marriage lasted for just five years after their retirement. Within a year, both of them got tired of traveling. Their plans for retirement had included nothing but expected good times. So, at 67, Tom opened a new decorating business, a business he had chosen at Alice's encouragement. She was quite artistic, and Tom had had a career in selling. The business seemed a logical choice.

But the business folded in less than two years, and during those years of squabbling over the business, Alice and Tom fell out of love. They took bankruptcy on the business, and, after the divorce, both remarried. Alice married a much older man, and he passed on soon after. I only know that Tom married a much younger woman. Retirement was definitely not the fun that the Hustons had expected.

Jade and Vera Levine planned their retirement carefully, but they didn't seem to fully understand how long retirement can last. They were anticipating a playful retirement. That is not necessarily a bad thing, but few of us can play for more than a year or two without losing the sense that our life is meaningful.

Jade and Vera learned quickly that they couldn't play for twenty to thirty years. Two years after retirement, Jade went back to his old job as a consultant. He had valuable, almost irreplaceable, wisdom in his field, and he stayed on at half-time and three-quarters pay for ten years.

Then Jade and Vera played for another year or so. Afterwards, Vera took on a great deal of volunteer work for the church. She was among the young-old, full of energy and people-oriented, and her life was full to overflowing. Jade started his private consulting business at 78. His office is in his home, and he is enjoying his work immensely.

All play does not always mean a satisfying retirement. In *Age Wave*, Ken Dychtwald and Joe Flower propose the following about balancing that play with something fulfilling:

> Since most older people would enjoy a chance to continue working but in a more flexible, less pressured fashion, the key to redefining retirement will lie in a restructuring of the way we work and the ease with which we are allowed to interweave work and nonwork throughout our adult years.[1]

Jade and Vera found a pattern of work and nonwork that worked for them, and the result has been a very satisfying retirement for both.

Emerging Patterns of After-Retirement Work

While some companies push employees toward retirement, many others suffer a serious loss of expertise when mandatory retirement rules force them to let valued employees go and still other employees decide to retire early. As a result, many companies are eager to accommodate the special needs of retired workers.

Retraining

Many workers are retiring early and voluntarily because they don't have the high-tech skills they need for their present work or further promotions. To counter this trend, many companies—including IBM and Ford—offer retraining. With special retraining, many employees continue to work, and many are able to move into new and different jobs.

Retraining is not exclusive to industry. Many individuals do their own retraining by going back to community colleges and technical schools for further education.

Some people choose to enter a totally new line of work. Most of us have been happy with our jobs, but we've always wanted to try something else. perhaps we'll pursue that long-held dream. Others of us have worked hard at hobbies throughout our lives, and now, with some retraining and refocusing, we can expand these hobbies into profitable business ventures.

For many people, making money is not a chief concern in post-retirement ventures. Dychtwald and Flower correctly point out that the goal after retirement is usually new experience rather than money. At the same time, though, most of us who take up second careers will feel invigorated by the new experiences only if our ventures are successful. And, perhaps unfortunately, making money has become the principal way of measuring success in our society.

Volunteerism

The world of health and social service would collapse without volunteer workers. Many elderly people are deeply involved in and committed to volunteer work. My wife, Ruth, refers to herself as a professional volunteer. Hospitals were the recipients of her dedicated work for many years, and now nursing homes are her focus.

Some people say that volunteers are not properly appreciated. That may or may not be your experience, but never doubt that your volunteer efforts are blessed by God and that you can be fulfilled by your work! Only in the frustrated minds of some unreasonable paid workers is volunteerism sometimes discredited. Please know that your volunteer work is a missionary work highly meaningful to you, a good example to others, and a faithful service to a needy world.

Retirement: Affluent and Otherwise

Statistics reveal that more than eighty-five percent of America's men and women over 65 do not work. This doesn't necessarily mean that they will never work again, but it does point to the fact that many highly affluent Americans move from affluent work lives to affluent retirement. In fact, there has been an explosion of retirement communities geared to affluence. Sun City near Phoenix, Arizona, is a prototype of these communities where age-segregated villages provide the elderly with an active lifestyle and excellent opportunities to socialize. Over one million retirees are now residing in such villages in Arizona, Florida, and California. For those who relish and can afford these lifestyles, there are few negatives. Self-esteem need not suffer because of relatively idle affluence, and there is no dearth of opportunities for affluent retirees to do the Lord's work in countless ways.

At the other end of the spectrum, many retirees need to supplement their Social Security income and retirement pensions if they are to meet their needs. For many of these people, to continue working is not only a boon to self-esteem, but it means being able to afford something a little more than the bare necessities.

Flextime

Some companies depend heavily on retirees for their part-time work force. Seasonal businesses, for instance, find it costly to keep a roster of full-time workers on hand. A large pool of part-time workers is more cost-effective.

Flextime allows workers to come when they want to or when they are needed. Granted, management faces the challenge of matching company needs with part-time workers' desires. However, many companies are very willing to allow great freedom to reliable and capable older workers who want to work a certain number of hours at certain times.

Flexplace

Some business enterprises have always allowed or even required employees to work at home. The drapery company which has decorated several houses for Ruth and me has always required their employees to work at home. Not only do workers choose the place, but they also determine when and how much they work.

Beware the Manipulators

Some employers solicit part-time work from the aging community and expect to pay a pittance for services. These unscrupulous entrepreneurs will take advantage of aging persons who must work in order to survive.

In contrast to this hateful reality are the many reputable companies which offer attractive situations to older folk. These companies work with their employees to determine when and where they will work—and these companies are often especially interested in their own retired workers.

All Work and No Play

Most of us are well aware of the workaholic personality, of Type A as opposed to Type B, and of some people's compulsive need to work, work, and work.

Retired people must seek to balance their needs, their desires, their leisure time, their social life, and their health concerns. The decision about how to live our retirement years is ours alone. I say let's maximize our lives! Let's work hard! Let's play hard! Let's be sure to watch the sun rise! Let's take the time to smell the roses. With Ulysses, let us say these words written by Alfred, Lord Tennyson:

> Come, my friends,
> 'Tis not too late to seek a newer world.
> Push off, and sitting well in order smite
> The sounding furrows; for my purpose holds
> To sail beyond the sunset, and the baths
> Of all the western stars, until I die.
> It may be that the gulfs will wash us down;
> It may be we shall touch the Happy Isles,
> And see the great Achilles, whom we knew.
> Though much is taken, much abides; and though
> We are not now that strength which in old days

Moved earth and heaven, that which we are, we are
One equal temper of heroic hearts,
Made weak by time and fate, but strong in will
To strive, to seek, to find, and not to yield.[2]

End-of-Chapter Questions

If you haven't retired, what plans have you made and what time frame have you outlined? If you have retired, how closely does the present match your plans and your dreams? What can you do to make your retirement more what you'd hoped it would be?

Who in your life is a good role model for retirement? Why do you think they are enjoying retirement? Talk to them about the secrets of success and learn from their answers.

Whom do you know who is disappointed or unhappy with retirement? Why do you think they feel this way? If you want, talk to them about their retirement and, again, learn from their answers.

What stages of retirement have you experienced and/or do you anticipate?

What has been/do you anticipate being the most rewarding aspect of retirement? What do you most enjoy about the present phase of your life, whether or not you are retired? At every age, we need to focus on the positives and the blessings of the present.

Endnotes

Chapter One

1. D. Blazer and E. Palmore, "Religion and Aging in a Longitudinal Panel," *The Gerontologist,* pp. 82-84 and D. O. Moberg, "Religiosity in Old Age," *The Gerontologist,* pp. 78-87.

2. S. C. Ainlay and D. R. Smith, "Aging and Religious Participation," *Journal of Gerontology,* pp. 357-363.

3. J. W. Fowler, *Stages of Faith* (New York: Harper and Row.

Chapter Two

1. E. Palmore, *Social Patterns in Normal Aging: Findings from the Duke Longitudinal Study* (Durham, N.C.: Duke University Press.

Chapter Three

1. Eric R. Kingson, Barbara A. Hirshorn, and John M. Cornman, *Ties That Bind* (Washington, DC: Seven Locks Press, 1986).

Chapter Five

1. Erik Erikson, *Identity, Youth and Crisis* (New York: W. W. Norton, 1968).

2. B. L. Neugarten, "Personality and Aging" in *The Handbook of the Psychology of Aging* (New York: Nostrand Reinhold, 1977).

Chapter Six

1. J. F. Fries and L. M. Crapo, *Vitality and Aging* (San Francisco: W. H. Freeman and Company).

Chapter Nine

1. Ken Dychtwald and Joe Flower, *Age Wave* (Los Angeles: Jeremy P. Tarcher, Inc., 1989).
2. Eric Berne, *Games That People Play* (New York: Grove Press, 1964).

Chapter Ten

1. E. Cumming and W. E. Henry, *Growing Old* (New York: Basic Book, 1961).

Chapter Eleven

1. K. W. Schaie, ed. *Longitudinal Studies in Adult Psychological Development* (New York: Guilford Press, 1983).
2. M. Elsayed, A. H. Ishmail, and R. S. Young, "Intellectual Differences of Adult Men Related to Age and Physical Fitness Before and After an Exercise Program," *Journal of Gerontology,* 35, (1940), pp. 383-387.
3. K. W. Schaie and A. Parham, "Stability of Adult Personality Traits: Fact or Fable?," *Journal of Personality and Social Psychology,* 34, pp. 146-158.
4. Gribben et al., "Complexity of Life Styles and Maintenance of Intellectual Abilities," *Journal of Social Issues,* 26, no. 2, pp. 47-61.

Chapter Fourteen

1. Dychtwald and Flower.
2. Alfred, Lord Tennyson, *The Norton Anthology of Literature,* vol. II, ed. M. H. Abrams, pp. 841-843.